Earning Your Wings

Earning Your Wings

William L. Coleman

BETHANY HOUSE PUBLISHERS

MINNEAPOLIS, MINNESOTA 55438

A Division of Bethany Fellowship, Inc.

Scripture verses marked TLB are taken from The Living Bible, copyright 1971 by Tyndale House Publishers, Wheaton, Ill. Used by permission.

Photo credits: Dick Easterday and Gary Johnson

ISBN 0–87123–311–8

Published by Bethany House Publishers
A Division of Bethany Fellowship, Inc.
6820 Auto Club Road, Minneapolis, MN 55438

Printed in the United States of America

BILL COLEMAN, well known for his devotional books for families, has been a pastor, is the father of three teenagers, and teaches in seminars and other speaking engagements. The majority of his time is now spent writing, with a long list of best-selling books to his credit. He and his family make their home in Aurora, Nebraska.

Other Teen Devotionals from Bethany House Publishers

The Great Date Wait and Other Hazards, William Coleman

If God Loves Me, Why Can't I Get My Locker Open?, Lorraine Peterson

Falling Off Cloud Nine and Other High Places, Lorraine Peterson

Why Isn't God Giving Cash Prizes?, Lorraine Peterson

Winning Isn't Always First Place, Dallas Groten

Doorways to Discipleship, Winkie Pratney

Handbook for the Followers of Jesus, Winkie Pratney

Youth Aflame, Winkie Pratney

Table of Contents

Life on the Move

When a family has teenagers in the home, parents and kids both see how quickly life is changing. One day it's dirt bikes, the next day it's girls, and later it's loud cars. With our June, it's mirrors, mad crushes, long phone calls, hairstyles and tape decks. She can't decide which is more important: eye shadow or sweat socks.

Change adds sparkle to life and makes each day different.

But that is only one side of being a teenager. Change is also bewildering, a bit frightening and just a notch too fast. It leaves many young people confused. They know they aren't children, and yet they aren't sure they are adults.

The letters in this book were written to help my teenagers think through that rapid change. These pages don't have all the answers, but hopefully they provide some helpful guidelines. Given some suggestions, most teenagers think well for themselves.

I hope each chapter will give both young adults and their parents some help in meeting these rapid changes.

William L. Coleman
Aurora, Nebraska

Who Is in Your Mirror?

Dear June,

Who was that person you saw in your mirror today? Almost every day you see someone slightly different. One day you may notice something has changed about your eyes. The next time you might see your nose differently. And it's really tough when you find a rude pimple has popped up on your cheek. That day can be awfully long because you feel as if everyone is staring right at the dreadful thing.

Mirrors are amazing at this stage of your life. You are going through rapid changes and it's hard to know what will show up next. One morning the mirror seems to point out your good looks and irresistible charm. The next day you feel like a squished mosquito.

All of us have gone through this; and while it doesn't help much to know that fact, one thing might: *You are normal.* If you feel your ears are too big, you're normal. If you think your hair looks like burnt spaghetti, you're normal.

Keep looking for the good points. They are there even when you think they aren't. Someday the changes will slow down and you will see the real you.

You may often forget this, but good looks are really not very elusive. Good looks come from a happy sparkle in your eyes. Good looks come from a friendly smile. Good looks are created by a caring sound in your voice. Attractiveness is a healthy sense of humor. The really sharp person takes time to listen to what others want to say. The Bible tells us, "Don't be concerned about the outward beauty that depends on jewelry, or beautiful clothes, or hair arrangement. Be beautiful inside, in your hearts, with the lasting charm of a gentle and quiet spirit which is so precious to God" (1 Pet. 3:3, 4, TLB).

None of us wants to look ugly, but some of us become that way. We are ugly when we are mean, short-tempered, unfair or hateful.

You can't beat good looks. And I've never met a kind person who didn't look good.

Love,
Dad

Something to Think About:

1. Who among your friends has the friendliest smile and kindest eyes?
2. Whom do you like to be with most? Why?
3. Do you know someone who thinks she looks good, but her personality is not?

So Long, Mary

Dear June,

The first summer Mary worked at camp seemed particularly hard for you. We could see you had missed her when she came home on the weekends. You fought for her time and seemed hurt when she went out for the evening with someone else.

We didn't realize how much all of the changes were affecting you. As parents we see so many rapid changes in our own lives that we don't always realize the upheavals upset you, too. The death of your grandmother, the graduation of your sister, your entrance into high school, the growing independence of your brother—all of them touched you. Some of the changes came too quickly and we didn't take time to discuss them.

Mary's empty nest has cost you a close friend, someone to bounce ideas off and to trade with. She was someone to talk to about the boy who didn't look at you—or the boy who did.

Even though you sometimes can't stand each other's ideas and will argue, I think that's mostly surface noise. There were also the hours when you sat at the drive-in, played tennis or talked in the evenings. Mary has traveled down the roads you now face and although you may want to travel them for yourself, it's helpful to talk to someone who knows where the bends and curves are.

Now that Mary is at college, the telephone and the mail seem to have become more important to you. I know it's not the same as having her here, but at least this offers some help and some friendship. I think it makes Mary feel great to know that you are remaining a part of each other's lives. It looks like a very good relationship.

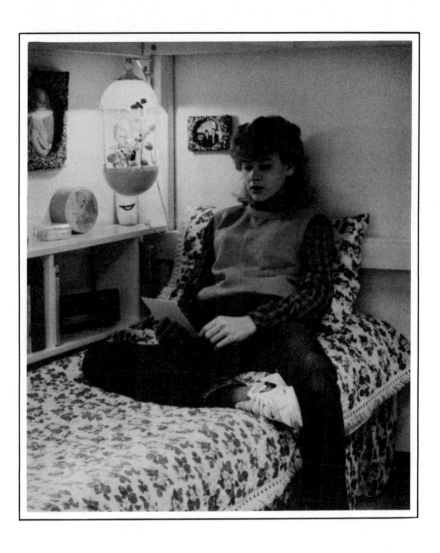

All of us need people to whom we can talk. We can become confused talking to ourselves and seeing life only through our own eyes. Someone who has been where you are and is also a good listener can help you across the rough spots.

I think many people would have avoided trouble if they had the right person to talk with at the right time. You are an independent person with a mind of your own. You are also smart enough to know that you need people to share ideas with.

"The good man asks advice from friends; the wicked plunge ahead—and fall" (Prov. 12:26, TLB).

Love,
Dad

Something to Think About:

1. What changes have been hard for you? What changes were good for you in the long run?
2. Have you ever had a close friend move away? Did you have anyone with whom you could talk it over?
3. Whom do you talk things over with?

The Total Haircut

Dear Jim,

Congratulations on your new haircut. It's daring, but some of the best fun in life is to launch out and be different.

Frankly, I didn't completely realize what we were getting into, but it turned out all right. When you asked if I'd mind if you got a crew cut, I said okay, but I didn't realize you were going to get one. It was just one of those things I say yes to because I think you're bluffing.

You proved it wasn't idle talk. The double shock for me came when your friend, instead of a barber, gave you the haircut. You took a huge chance. What if your friend had messed it up, making you look like singed chicken?

It turned out great. You tiptoed on the fence, balancing yourself between what your parents would accept and what they would not. Good job. At your age you need to reach out and try new things. That's part of breaking away and becoming independent.

We were proud of your determination. You got your hair cut your way and you didn't care whether or not others did it. It's easy to admire that kind of spirit. That's the attitude that invents new machines, discovers new medicines and initiates new ministries.

To be honest, we were happy to see some other boys soon get their hair cut the same way. I guess we want you to be different but not ridiculous. It means we want you to break away but not too far.

Your haircut was part of a total picture. How far can you go? How soon can you make decisions on your own? When do you have to ask your parents and when don't you?

I don't have any easy answers for these questions.

No magic formulas. You, your mother and I will have to learn together. No two children are the same. No two parents are the same. Probably no two children pull away from the parents in exactly the same way.

The one thing we've learned is that you need to cut the strings. Sometimes you cut too many too fast and you send us scrambling for the aspirin. The next time we overreact and leave you beating your head on your bedroom wall.

Somehow it all works out. We learn, you learn, and hopefully we arrive at independence at just the right time.

Thanks for being such an interesting person. It's fun to cut strings together.

We have a great deal to learn from each other. I hope we both keep our ears open.

"For he wanted them to be understanding, just and fair in everything they did" (Prov. 1:3, TLB).

Love,
Dad

Something to Think About:

1. When your parents allow you certain independence, do they take it away later? Should they if you showed you couldn't handle it?
2. What do you think your parents should allow you to do that they won't? How can you convince them you are ready for the responsibility?
3. What is the hardest roadblock in cutting strings?

Being Popular

Dear June,

There was a boy in our high school who worked hard at being popular. He was one of the few car owners in our school, bought the best clothes, tried to be everywhere. In the long run people did not seem to care for him. He worked hard to be popular but he forgot to be himself. People felt he was always pretending.

A recent survey seems to support this fact. Often the busiest young people are the loneliest. They are flying here and there, but they fail to take time to develop any meaningful relationships.

It feels great to get along with a lot of people. Most of us would like to have some popularity. However, it is the deep, dependable friendships that really count. It is possible to know many people without knowing anyone.

You seem to have both popularity and close friends. Your wide circle of friends gives your life variety and interest. Fortunately, you also have that smaller circle of close, almost daily friends. They are the ones you can count on when you need them.

It's your life, your style and your values, but try to keep a few suggestions in mind. For instance, remember not to sacrifice a handful of good friends for a thousand people you barely know. Try not to confuse popularity with being around a lot of people or being invited to a great many parties. That is activity but not necessarily friendship.

A famous singer once said she was loved by 20,000 people at a concert but afterward went home totally alone. She was popular but that didn't mean she had friends.

It's far better for you to be faithful to your true

friends than to chase popularity. If you have many good friends, that's great; however, that doesn't come by going after it.

Try concentrating on two things: be relaxed and enjoy yourself, and be a dependable and true friend.

If you chase after popularity, you might begin to treat people like stepping-stones. The people you think help you grow in popularity will be the only ones you have around. Those who are of less "social standing" will have to be discarded.

Those are the attitudes that create cliques. We shut out people who fail to rise up to our imaginary standard. Cliques are ugly, disease-infested sewers. Close friendships are healthy; cliques are cruel.

If you have to aim for popularity or steady friends, the choice ought to be obvious to you.

"Never abandon a friend—either yours or your father's" (Prov. 27:10, TLB).

Love,
Dad

Something to Think About:

1. What qualities make good friendships? Explain.
2. Have you known someone who is popular but for whom you had no respect? Why?
3. Have you known anyone who would cheat to get votes?

Why Weren't You Born Rich?

Dear June,

This question probably occurs to all of us sooner
or later. It looks like it would have been just as
simple for us to have been born into a bigger home,
have a few better cars; even a servant to clean up our
room would be fun.

What would you do if you were rich? Would you
wear a white fur coat? Would you jet down to "Worlds
of Fun" or simply build an amusement park in your
backyard? I'm sure you would install a private
telephone in your room the very first thing.

Before our dreams carry us away, let me share
some news with you. We are rich. Not as materially
wealthy as the Rockefellers or the DuPonts, but we
are definitely rich.

In the United States, salaries last year were higher
than those in 70% of the world. The average income
in Haiti last year was between $200 and $600. This
means most of their people are born, grow up and die
on a dirt floor.

The illnesses you and I are treated for regularly
can end lives in other countries. There frequently are
no doctors or medicines available. People can go blind,
become crippled or die for simple lack of medical
attention.

I'm not trying to send you on a guilt trip, but once
in a while we need to be called back to reality. We
are not as rich as many others, but we are wealthier
than most of the world.

Practically everyone daydreams about luxury. We
are overwhelmed by the high living we see and read
about. If you watch television commercials, the ads
make it look as if we should have private jets,
limousines, and a summer place in Tahiti.

Commercials add a lot to our general discontent and greed. However, they are not the sole source. Greed has been around much longer than television.

It is far more important to be content with ourselves and God than to lust after riches. If we are not at peace and happy with ourselves, no amount of wealth can make us that way.

A former President said that money is important only if you don't have it. Once you get it you realize how little difference it makes in the total picture. Seriously try thinking about that.

Greed has no end. If we long for what others have, we will always want more.

The next time you are in your room, do yourself a favor and look around at what you have. Count your tops and jeans. Notice your furniture. Don't forget to smile once more in your mirror and see your straightened teeth. Then thank God again for giving you much more than you need.

I'm glad I know you. I always wanted to be related to someone who was wealthy.

"Not that I was ever in need, for I have learned how to get along happily whether I have much or little" (Phil. 4:11, TLB).

Love,
Dad

Something to Think About:

1. Do you think it is okay for a Christian to have a fancy home and several nice cars? Why or why not?
2. If you become wealthy, what will you do with your wealth?
3. How much of what we have should we give to someone less fortunate? What about people dying of starvation?

Choosing Friends

Dear June,

Today I heard about a teenage girl who was dropped by her friends. I didn't get all the details, but I know it hurts to get dumped. This is a painful reality of the world we live in. Sometimes you may wake up to discover your friends were not friends at all.

Have you ever watched someone who was shut out by a group? It reminds me of little children who say, "Let's not play with her." This is a form of prejudice, because people are saying they are better than someone else.

I remember playing a certain baseball game as a child, and suddenly someone pointed to the kid next to me and said, "He's dirty. I'm not going to play with him." The accuser then marched off the field. Often I've wondered how that made my friend feel. I'm sure it tore away his insides.

We make an awful mistake if we select our friends according to their clothing, looks, homes, cars or grades. None of those things tell us about the quality of the person, how much we can trust him or what his character is like.

Choosing friends is one of those personal areas that each young person basically controls. We parents may give you advice and tell you our impressions of your friends; we may warn you about a character flaw that disturbs us. But of course we don't know your friends as well as you do. You appreciate their good qualities—their faithfulness, their dependability. As parents we may see only the hairstyles, shoes and rumpled jackets. All we ask is that you choose your close friends wisely. Will they pull you up or down?

Often we parents seem to think young people should easily get along with each other. Once after we spent the evening with a family, Mary told us, "When you plan time with a family, don't always assume that the young people will get along. I'm not complaining, I just want to give you information."

It was a good lesson because often we assume that your age will naturally bring teens together.

Choosing friends is a magic domain that you must own for yourself. Collect friends who care. Collect friends who can give you a little wider outlook on life. Collect friends who don't have to pretend in order to impress you. Collect friends for a day. Collect them for a year. Collect them for a lifetime.

Collect friends who help you share the rich, rewarding parts of life.

"A true friend is always loyal" (Prov. 17:17, TLB).

Love,
Dad

Something to Think About:

1. Are there people in your class that are avoided because they are poor? How could you befriend them?
2. Have you ever been excluded? How did it feel?
3. How would Jesus treat the underdog?

Call of the Horns

Dear Jim,

We hear them practically every day. They sound to me like duck calls trying to lure unsuspecting game. What we're hearing are car horns as young people cruise by our house. If we are sitting at the table, we can see your eyes brighten. It's almost as if you are trying to imagine who it might be.

There is nothing like good friends who want to do things and go places with you. From the frequency of the horns, you must have a small army of friends. They are special and are some of the most important people in your life.

As parents, it's hard to tell one horn from the other. They all sound like good friends who want to say "hello." We know that when you're busy at home, working around the house, hearing the horns hurts you. We can almost see the pain in your face because you want to be with them.

It will probably always be that way. Some things must be done, but there is the temptation to drop our responsibilities and chase the immediate. All of us want to do that once in a while, but we need to learn to keep everything in place.

Frankly, a few of the horns worry me. I'm not sure where the young people want to go or what plans they have. That's where your good judgment will have to come in. All horns sound alike to parents. Young people have to decide which ones to listen to.

Every horn is an invitation to get away, to go and do something. But not every horn is good. You do an excellent job of following some horns and letting others pass. It shows a growing maturity.

The Bible says, "There are no horns except those that are common to man, but God is faithful, who will not let the horns become more than you can handle, but will with the horns also make a way to escape, that you may be able to withstand it" (1 Cor. 10:13, Coleman Free Translation).

Love,
Dad

Something to Think About:

1. Do your parents get to meet and know your friends? Should they?
2. What things do your friends do that you are not allowed to?
3. Can God help you choose what things to do? Be specific.

30

Do You Sometimes Feel Lonely?

Dear June,

What age group is the loneliest in our society? A person might guess it to be the elderly. But several surveys have proven that they may be the least lonely.

The loneliest age groups are teenagers. They appear to be the busiest and many of them laugh a great deal, but statistics from interviews indicate they are in last place.

Certainly all of us are lonely sometimes, but there are a few groups that hurt more than others. Of teenagers, girls seem to be lonelier than boys. And in some cases those who are the most active tend to be the loneliest. Just the fact that a person keeps moving doesn't necessarily mean he has meaningful friends.

Loneliness is a feeling. You can be alone in your

room and not be the least bit lonely. In fact, you might resent it if someone shows up. As an example you say, "The problem with having people over for the night is that they don't go home early enough the next day."

You seem to do a good job of fighting loneliness. You have several special, or "core," friends and you stay active enough to keep those friendships fresh. You also make new friends and pay the happy price of keeping those friendships alive.

However, you also seem capable of living with yourself. If there is no one around, you can make do. If you have a project to complete or something to make, you enjoy that time alone.

Yet, when you want people around, you know how to use the phone. You aren't afraid to call people, girls or boys, and get an activity going.

I think the people who suffer the most from loneliness are the ones waiting to be called.

Love,
Dad

Something to Think About:

1. How much time do you like to be alone each day?
2. When do you like to be with friends? After school? Evening? Other?
3. What is the best part of being with friends?

Looking for Guidance

Dear June,

All of us need someone to talk to once in a while. Your curling iron burns out, your pink sweater gets caught in your jacket zipper, or you discover that your sister used your homework to start the fire in the fireplace. Life can be tough. When it gets hard and confusing, it would be nice to have some place to turn.

Often you turn to your brother or sister, your friends and especially your mother. Another great source of practical guidance is your Bible. It contains wisdom from God and has stood the test of thousands of years. It's hard to beat advice that comes from God.

Granted, the Bible doesn't tell you whether or not to go out with a boy who wears a football helmet, orange tennis shoes and carries a stop sign. Common sense should take care of that one. However, the Bible has a lot to say about temptation, love, lust, forgiveness, laughter, sadness and other daily feelings. The Bible tells us about God, but it also guides us through the forest of life with all its fallen logs, deep holes and dark corners.

The apostle Paul tells us the Bible is an outstanding form of guidance. "The whole Bible was given to us by inspiration from God and is useful to teach us what is true and to make us realize what is wrong in our lives; it straightens us out and helps us do what is right" (2 Tim. 3:16, TLB).

Sometimes we need something to "make us realize what is wrong in our lives." At other times we need something to "help us do what is right." We may not need a miracle or to have God zap us somehow. We have to have our cloudy thinking cleared up. The Bible is great at clearing up cloudy heads.

As you read through the Bible, take special notice of the wisdom sections. David and Solomon went through years of hard knocks learning what they wrote in the Psalms and Proverbs. Jesus handles a carload of practical topics in His Sermon on the Mount (Matt. 5—7).

The next time you discover that your sister took your best sweater to college, you can recall what the Bible says about anger, forgiveness, sharing and sending her your blouse also. Your sister might even remember what the Bible says about stealing sweaters.

Love,
Dad

Something to Think About:

1. Do you read the Bible when you have a problem? Explain.
2. Has a Bible verse come to your mind when you wondered what to do? Explain.
3. Do you think reading the Bible would help you grow wiser. If so, in what way?

Finding Self-control

Dear June,

Most of us would like to do whatever we want.
Why do we have to be places on time? Why do we
have to keep a close check on our money? Why do we
have to obey traffic signs and laws?

It seems as if everyone is telling us what to do—
teachers, parents, police, brothers, sisters, coaches,
everyone but the dog catcher. Sometimes you wonder
why people don't just get off your back and leave you
alone.

I remember feeling like that as a teenager.
Sometimes I wondered if God specifically created
certain people to tell me what to do.

That was one of the reasons why I could hardly
wait to grow up. I wanted to be free, to run my own
life. I would tell myself when to go to bed, what to
eat, when to take the car, how to spend my money. I
knew there had to be that special age, that great
position in life when I would be free.

If there is that special age of freedom, I am still
looking for it. The banker tells me when to pay bills.
The police tell me where to park the car. My family
tells me when to be home for something. The mailman
tells me to shovel the walk. Even the trees tell me
when to rake the lawn.

That's life and we will always be told what to do.
As we grow older the people and the circumstances
change but the facts do not. There will always be
someone or something telling us what to do.

Don't let that depress you. Life is still enjoyable.
However, the controls that are put on by others never
completely go away.

I think the closest we ever come to real freedom
hinges on a decision we can make. Do we want to

control ourselves, or do we want others to control us? I believe self-control is as close as we get to freedom.

For instance, if I stop mowing my lawn, the city will eventually send out a crew, cut my grass and fine me for it. If I drive our car across other people's lawns, the police will arrest me. The best freedom I have is the freedom of self-control.

The writer of Proverbs put it directly:

"A man without self-control is as defenseless as a city with broken-down walls" (25:28, TLB).

If I can't control myself, I am open to the control of others. Someone is going to tell me what to do. It might as well be me.

Love,
Dad

Something to Think About:

1. How do you rate yourself?
   a. Always obey regulations
   b. Generally obey regulations
   c. Obey only when forced
   d. Try to find ways around regulations
2. Do you think most school rules were made because students couldn't exercise self-control?
3. Would most people be happier if they had a stronger self-control? Why or why not?

Giving Up a Concert

Dear Jim,

Thanks for giving up the concert. It was probably a serious sacrifice on your part, but it was one that needed to be made. So many of your friends were planning to go to the concert that it must have hurt you to miss it. You showed great maturity in the way you handled it.

Your cousins don't come here to Nebraska often. This state isn't exactly the tourist capital of the world. That made it even more important to stick around when they came.

Naturally you didn't like it when we said you couldn't go, but your reaction was stable. No fits or pouting. You suggested some alternatives but we vetoed each one. From that moment on we didn't hear one agonizing complaint. Congratulations! That tells us a lot.

Sometimes you don't feel like you are part of the family life. You are growing up and finding interests of your own. We don't have the same togetherness we had when you were a child. We shouldn't expect that. However, there are times when we need to cooperate. We cooperate for the good of our family and others around us.

For us, togetherness means you enjoy doing things with your family. That can't always be true at your age. Cooperation means you go along with it whether you like it or not. Cooperation shows clear signs of maturity. It means you don't have to have your own way.

When someone refuses to do something unless he likes it, he needs to grow up. Life is flooded with activities we don't particularly enjoy.

You made the most of the situation and seemed to

have a good time with your younger cousins. You certainly went out of your way to make them happy.

Thanks again. I think you are growing up great.

"The selfish man quarrels against every sound principle of conduct by demanding his own way" (Prov. 18:1, TLB).

Love,
Dad

Something to Think About:

1. Is some member of your family especially good at being thoughtful of others?
2. What do you enjoy doing most with your family?
3. Are you allowed to express your wishes to your parents?

A Borrowed Blouse

Dear June,

You don't get angry often, but when you do we all know about it. And sometimes it's difficult to blame you for getting mad. When you find something of yours has been taken, it's hard to keep your cool.

Few things seem to upset you more than to have your sister borrow one of your blouses. This is especially true if she does not ask permission. And equally disturbing if you were counting on wearing it that day.

When you discover it missing, it is everyone to her battle station. Voices are sky high, both of you are stomping around. You accuse each other of trespasses that happened three years ago. If we don't want to get yelled at, we just stay out of the way.

All of it is understandable and all of it is unnecessary. There are some rules of common decency that would prevent these mini-riots. Let's look at a few of them.

Do unto sisters what you would have sisters do unto you.

If you take clothes, radios, tapes and curling irons without first asking, you are inviting your sister to do the same. That has been the problem. If you want her to stop doing this, you must be willing to stop first.

Set down some rules for borrowing.

You are near enough in size that you like to borrow from each other. Each of you has something the other wants. Together you should agree on ways to borrow.

Do you need to be asked first? Would you like to have a note, describing what was borrowed, left on your desk? Are there certain things she can feel free to borrow but not other things? A friendly discussion on how to borrow would happily stop these arguments. It also might get you some use of a few more of her things.

When in doubt, try kindness.

Try not to allow every incident to throw you into an uproar. All of us make mistakes, forget to ask and forget to return things. Patience, forgiveness, and generosity will work miraculously among brothers and sisters.

These are simply three suggestions. You are creative enough to think of other guidelines. The great part is that it gives you a sensible way to borrow. And the greater part for your parents is that it is easier on their nerves.

"Do for others what you want them to do for you" (Matt. 7:12, TLB).

Love,
Dad

Something to Think About:

1. What is one good rule for borrowing that works for you?
2. Should one borrow money?
3. Have you had a bad experience with borrowing or lending?

Saying "I'm Sorry"

Dear Jim,

If we could do it over, there are a few decisions I would like to take back. Sometimes we were too strict with you and other times we weren't strict enough. Either extreme is unfair to you. I'm sorry we didn't call all the shots correctly but we tried our best.

None of us is fair all of the time. I think the hard part is to face our mistakes and tell someone we are sorry. To admit we are wrong might sound like a form of weakness.

Saying "I'm sorry" isn't really a weakness. Those who cannot say it have to remain rigid even after they know they have made a mistake. Often then they will have to cover up or stretch their story or even lie in order to make themselves look good. And I'm not talking about young people alone; adults can be guilty of protecting themselves from an obvious error.

Being sorry and saying so is an art well worth mastering. We don't want to throw apologies around like candy. It becomes meaningless if we say it when we have done nothing wrong. However, an honest, clear, crisp "I'm sorry" can earn us tons of respect from the person to whom we say it.

Being able to admit our errors says we are relaxed with ourselves. We don't have to be in a mad frenzy to hide our mistakes. All of us mess up from time to time.

Saying "I'm sorry" certainly beats trying to make up stories when we are late getting home. There is usually tension, some distrust and plenty of questions. A brief "I'm sorry I stayed later than I should have" will sound much better to an adult. Hopefully when your parents make a mistake they will give you the same honest reply.

None of us likes to be wrong, yet at times all of us are. Admitting that we were wrong is an act of courage.

Maybe we can help each other own up to our mistakes and grow from them.

"I confess my sins; I am sorry for what I have done" (Ps. 38:18, TLB).

Love,
Dad

Something to Think About:

1. Have you said, "I'm sorry" within the last two weeks?
2. Can you remember when "I'm sorry" cleared up a potentially bad situation?
3. Do you know anyone who is right all the time and never needs to say "I'm sorry"?

Handling Criticism

Dear June,

Do you hate being told what to do? Parents may seem to have an endless list of corrections. Sit up! Chew your food! Don't run in the house! Did you make your bed? Where are you going? When will you be back? Get the cat out of the house!

Taking criticism isn't easy to do. As you grow older you may begin to think it should end. After all, adults aren't supposed to be criticized.

That's a mistake. Adults are often given criticism. Bosses, wives, children, friends and parking lot attendants tell us what to do.

We don't enjoy criticism, but our ability to listen to it and respond kindly says a great deal about our maturity.

There was an excellent baseball player in Detroit who had an outstanding career. Despite his obvious ability, there was one thing he could not handle well and that was criticism. If the manager told him to tighten up his batting grip, he wouldn't show up the next day. If a sports columnist said he wasn't trying hard enough, the player wouldn't talk to anyone for weeks. The slightest hint that he wasn't perfect sent him into hiding.

A great amount of talent was wasted because he could not learn to deal with criticism.

We have given you a lot of criticism over the years. Frankly, we owe you an apology for criticizing you too much. And for getting on your case for little things that didn't mean anything. Sometimes we were simply trying too hard to make that "wonderful you" shine through.

Another thing we should apologize for is not criticizing you enough. Some things we let go and failed to mention when we should have helped more. Criticism is an art and we have not mastered it perfectly.

We also need to thank you. Your timely, polite criticism has been an enormous help to us. You have shown us when things have been neglected or pushed way out of proportion.

Criticizing parents is a risky business. However, most of the time you have delivered it carefully and discreetly.

Each of us is in the process of growing. As we learn to accept and evaluate criticism, we come closer to maturity.

"It is a badge of honor to accept valid criticism" (Prov. 25:12, TLB).

Love,
Dad

Something to Think About:

1. Is it hard for you to accept criticism? Why?
2. What should you do if the criticism isn't deserved?
3. How should you treat people who criticize everything?

Drawing Lines

Dear Jim,

Without lines on the highways, I wouldn't be too
thrilled about driving. I can imagine that everyday
driving would turn into something like a bumper car
rally. So I am definitely happy we have those lines
as guides.

I'm equally glad that the rest of life has guidelines.
For example, without the law of gravity we might
shake pepper into our eyes, and we would have a hard
time walking downstairs.

Generally, teenagers enjoy having their parents
draw a few lines, set up a few rules and establish
some laws. They may not like to admit it, but despite
this denial many teenagers have felt more secure
because their parents stood between them and a
difficult situation.

Many times a young person has been spared great
pain because he was forced to obey his parents. I
think God understood this need when He had Paul
record: "Children, obey your parents; this is the right
thing to do because God has placed them in authority
over you" (Eph. 6:1, TLB).

Sometimes the group has invited you to do
something that you feel is wrong. It's a place where
you feel you don't belong. And yet, it's hard to say no
because you might look chicken to refuse.

In those hours when it's hard for a teenager to
make up his mind, it's good to have his parents step
in. They say no for him. More than once a teenager
has felt relieved that someone stepped in. He doesn't
usually admit that and will probably still protest in
untranslatable mumblings.

However, after the storm dies down, the young
person will actually feel good inside. It's almost like a

rescue. Maybe he can't express it, but once in a while he is thankful for parents who draw lines.

Love,
Dad

Something to Think About:

1. Exercise: Go to your room, close the door, practice saying *no* aloud firmly and with meaning many times.
2. Exercise: Say thank you to your parents sometime for keeping you from getting into trouble.
3. Does your circle of friends help you or hurt you in the kind of activities they choose?

Don't Miss Jesus

Dear June,

Among all of the church ceremonies, services and rituals, be sure and do yourself a favor: don't miss Jesus. It's easy to become a follower of groups, clubs and even study groups without getting down to the important issue. Jesus Christ, the Son of God, is worth getting to know.

See Jesus as the human being. When He was a young person, Christ must have talked to girls, lived with brothers and sisters, done jobs, gone to class and some days felt sad. He knew His parents didn't always understand Him.

All of that is important because Jesus knows exactly how you feel. He was tempted, He was hurt, He was happy. And yet Jesus refused sin.

Also, get to know Jesus as the unequaled Son of God. He holds the door to heaven. He understands the mind of God and He understands the mind of teenagers. Because you trust in Him, you have a place with God forever.

June, there are many questions about religion that are tough to handle. That's why it's important to get to know Christ well.

Speaking of Christ, Heb. 4:15 says: "This High Priest of ours understands our weaknesses, since he had the same temptations we do, though he never once gave way to them and sinned" (TLB).

Love,
Dad

Something to Think About:

1. What person do you know that Jesus is important to?
2. How do you get to know Jesus personally?
3. How can you share your faith in Jesus?

A Time to Speak Up

Dear June,

In some ways life is a game and the smart people learn how to play it. I call the game "What to do when and when to back off?" Wealthy businessmen, teachers, truck drivers, nurses, as well as husbands and wives, all learn the game.

Children can learn it at an early age and perfect it by the time they grow up. Those who fail at this game receive a great many bumps on their heads.

For a young person the rules are fairly simple. There is a right time to ask a parent and a wrong time. There is a correct time to share bad news and a time to hold back that news.

You're sharp enough to have learned most of these. A bad time to ask Dad for something might be the minute he comes in the door in the evening: If you wait until he can relax a while, you may find him more open to your ideas.

Mothers operate on the same principle. When she's bringing in groceries is a bad time to ask for a raise in allowance. If dinner is running late, you might consider waiting to tell her that the cat got into the fishbowl.

You do well at this. I think parents are often like orchestras and you seem to play them with a minimum of squeaks. It takes practice but through time you have learned to wield the baton wisely.

If you could put the principle into a nutshell it reads, "A time to be quiet, a time to speak up" (Eccles. 3:7, TLB).

Another guideline that seems to work well is to try not to give bad news late at night. People get tired, and their emotional and physical resources are normally running low. However, sometimes it's an ideal time for a friendly discussion or sharing good ideas.

We need to be just as aware of your low ebbs. After school, practice and piano lessons, you come home having put in a hard ten-hour day. That's no time for us to bring up complaints. We are trying to learn to be more thoughtful and respectful of your feelings.

I wish we could keep our cool all the time. You do a great job trying to hold onto yours.

Love,
Dad

Something to Think About:

1. When is the best time to talk to Mom? to Dad?
2. When is the best time for them to talk to you?
3. Do you have family conferences in your house?

Respect for Each Other

Dear Jim,

Most teenagers come to the place where they think parents are in total darkness. If you are there now, don't feel surprised. It comes and goes.

Low tide is usually around 15 or 16. You are reaching for adulthood. Suddenly it looks as if your parents don't know much about fun, clothes, food, television, friends, dating or education.

With most teenagers the feeling will last for years. The young person has discovered that his parents don't know everything. Now he imagines that his parents don't know anything.

Sometimes it may look as if one of your parents knows almost nothing. Most often this is the parent who tends to give most of the orders.

This pattern is true because it is part of growing up. While you are trying out your wings and learning to fly for yourself, you don't want your parents to get in your way. Sometimes you may feel the best way to ignore your parents is to pretend they don't know anything.

I think you're going through some of these feelings now. It can be a hard time because parents and teenagers can feel themselves pulling apart. Pulling apart is painful—for both parents and youth.

Try to keep in mind that this is a phase. It is a normal, even healthy, part of growing up. The good news is that it passes. Usually after high school or sometimes a little later, most young people regain an even greater appreciation for their parents.

If you sometimes feel a distance between us, or if sometimes you feel angry toward us, it is easy to understand. Those feelings don't change our basic love for each other.

During the hard times we will try to maintain our respect for one another. And when the conflicts calm down we will probably find ourselves closer than ever.

"And this is the promise: that if you honor your father and mother, yours will be a long life, full of blessing" (Eph. 6:3, TLB).

Love,
Dad

Something to Think About:

1. Do your friends think their parents don't know anything?
2. What can teens do to get along better with parents?
3. What can parents do to get along better with teens?

Educate Your Parents

Dear Jim,

The world has changed since I was 16. We didn't have air conditioning; we watched Captain Video on black and white TV and our idea of a wild movie was Marlon Brando with a torn tee shirt.

Some things we considered all-absorbing as teens have faded now. The thrill of winning a softball game has been replaced for us by a computer problem at work. Going out with friends has been replaced with a quiet evening at home.

Because we've changed, it's hard to understand how young people feel. We have trouble knowing what's important to a teenager.

That is why a parent needs teenagers. The teen can educate them about the world he lives in. It does not need to be a speech, a lecture or a sermon. He merely needs to share some of his feelings as a young person.

What does a modern teenager call fun? Where does he like to go? What does he do after the A & W drive-in closes? (I assume it does close.) Whose house does he go to to watch television? What kind of clothes does he consider important?

We parents don't know it all. That isn't necessarily our fault. We can't move in an adult society and be teenagers at the same time. If we tried, you would quickly lose respect for us.

Share your teen years with your parents. They need to know about cars, clothing, styles and teachers. Don't tell them everything at once but drop a little information here and there.

There are certain tricks to educating parents. For maximum value avoid a few turn-off phrases. Such as:

"Everybody's getting them." A red flag will go up. Try giving them names.

"Everybody's going." A genuine no. Try here to be specific.

"Nobody comes home that early." Paint a clear picture for your parents. What will you do until that hour? Who will you be with? Where will you be?

Parents want you to have certain freedoms as long as you both know what the boundaries are. Do your parents and yourself a favor by filling in as many of the blanks as possible.

Traditionally parents are slow to learn the way of the younger generation. Know that love and sharing will close that gap.

In the long run, everyone is the winner. The parent is introduced into the world of youth and the teenager gains greater freedom. Thanks for being my teacher.

Love,
Dad

Something to Think About:

1. Do your parents understand that certain styles are important?
2. Has it been easy for you to talk to your parents?
3. What are some of the things you can share with your parents?

When Parents Grow Older

Dear June,

As parents have grown older, most have lost the high energy level that you have. They find that their bodies are not as agile and quick as they once were. About the time you want to see the countryside, your parents are conked out for an afternoon nap.

However, despite the age difference there are times when you would like to do some things together. You can still share life and a few of its activities. One way to do things together is to aim for events that would interest them.

For instance, your parents will still play football, hit fly balls, throw Frisbees and take some of the longest walks known to man. Just because they don't want to sunbathe or watch boys at the park doesn't mean there aren't things you can do together.

I believe there are several things that keep parents and their teenagers from doing more together. One of the biggest problems is that many young people don't want to be seen with their parents. It's all right to admit that, because parents may not always want to be seen with their teenagers. The fact is, we are often apart because of choice. Many teenagers feel it makes them look like children to be with their parents. This is no one's fault, just reality.

Another major hurdle is the reluctance to compromise. Adults and young people must give in and do what the other wants. It's called sharing. It's called communicating.

A large number of parents would be happy to shoot baskets with their teenagers. They would enjoy fishing off a pier on a warm evening. Parents may not be as energetic as you are, but that doesn't mean they won't want to join you in some activities.

When you want to play some tennis with your mother, simply ask her. It might surprise you how willing she is. If you want me outside, bounding around, get me a baseball glove and dare me to hit fly balls. If I'm careful it won't even throw my back out.

By making the first move, you are telling a parent you want to do something with him and are willing to do it on his level. That opens an avenue of communication, and the next time he can do something you will enjoy more.

Too many parents and young people have given up on each other.

There is a good middle ground. You aren't in your forties, and I can't be a teenager again. Thank heavens! I'll keep my graying hair (slightly). I've earned it. But this gray head will still play ball with you.

"White hair is a crown of glory and is seen most among the godly" (Prov. 16:31, TLB).

Love,
Dad

Something to Think About:

1. Name one thing you have done recently with your parents that you enjoyed.
2. How do you and your parents agree on an activity you will do together?
3. Do you want to do things with parents more often? What sort of things?

Family Conferences

Dear Jim,

Some young people say they don't like family conferences. I think that's because it reminds them that they are responsible to a family. Being a family means we have to give and take and sometimes follow orders. Most of that sounds fairly stifling when you are a teenager.

Despite the admittedly distasteful aspects, family conferences can be a help if you learn how to handle them correctly. You can make them work for you by simply giving them a little thought.

A family conference is a good time to collect information: what is being planned, what are you planning, what are the alternatives. It gives you a chance to think ahead and put in a good word for what you want. Without a family conference parents will usually just lay down laws and make announcements. That leaves you on the outside waiting to be told what to do.

Conferences are also opportunities for teenagers to give input. Too often young people hurt themselves by throwing these opportunities away. They clam up and freeze over trying to get the message across that they don't like family conferences. Unfortunately that is the only message they get across.

Sooner or later a father will scan the room and say the traditional, "Now, what do you think, son?" Nine times out of ten son stares at the floor and rubs his torn tennis shoe into the carpet.

That's a waste. Inside himself the young person probably has a point he would like to get out. The chance to express himself is laid wide open like a sliced watermelon. But instead of being heard, the young person imitates a cement block.

Family conferences aren't ideal, but they beat silence anytime. With some of us it isn't that we don't have a chance to talk, but rather that we don't take advantage of that chance.

If you want to get in a few words about how you feel, speak up when the opportunity is there.

Love,
Dad

Something to Think About:

1. Do you like family conferences? Why or why not?
2. How would you improve family conferences?
3. Are your suggestions ever taken and changes made? Explain.

Let's Keep Talking

Dear Jim,

Sometimes things get tense at our house. Maybe you took the car without asking and I'm really upset. Later, I find you did ask your mother and there was nothing to get riled over.

Another time you came in late and we were pacing the floor. Parents and young people seem to go through these gyrations often. Who promised what? Did we communicate? Are we each trying to guess what the other one meant?

After fighting many battles due to poor communication, I've decided a lot of harm can be avoided by more direct, clear talking. If I feel there is a misunderstanding, the best solution for me is to ask you about it. Or if something is bugging me, I need to bring it up. Letting things slide only seems to result in more confusion and pent-up anger. And the sooner we deal with a situation the more quickly we can clear it up and move on to happier matters.

Once we stop talking we begin building walls. The longer we go without talking, the higher and thicker those walls become. Walls shut out and create distance. Walls promote fear, uncertainty and distrust.

I know what it's like to not want to talk. It usually happens when I feel sorry for myself. I think that if someone is going to act a certain way, I won't have anything to do with him. It's wrong for me to do this.

Not talking is a form of rejection. It says, "Stay away from me. I don't want you." All of us may do this once in a while.

The last thing we need to do is reject each other. We have differences and we should learn to respect those. But differences should not lead to rejection, because rejection can only damage.

I especially appreciate the days when you make the extra effort to talk. I know it isn't easy. People of all ages have trouble communicating, especially when they disagree. However, many times you stick in there and let your feelings be made known.

Thanks for talking. It helps keep a good relationship between you and your parents.

Love,
Dad

Something to Think About:

1. How do you handle who uses the car at your house?
2. List some ways of being more friendly. Pick one and put it into action today.
3. Do you know someone who clams up when he disagrees? What suggestions do you have for him?

We All Get Angry

Dear June,

I know a man who seems to be angry all the time. Whether you mention politics, the weather, cars or God, you get the same disgusted reaction from him. I have often wondered if he is really that hostile at life or if he is just putting on an act.

Occasionally a young person will act the same way and will seem sour on life itself. For this person nothing works—school isn't fair, his parents don't understand, everything is depressing.

It's a sad way to waste so many good years. There are too many mountains to climb, too many canyons to explore, too many people to meet, too much to enjoy to merely sit around being miserable.

All of us get angry sometimes. That makes good sense since there are injustices that call for emotion and often action. But there probably aren't as many injustices as we imagine. Smart people reserve their anger for the times when it is really important.

"A wise man restrains his anger and overlooks insults. This is to his credit" (Prov. 19:11, TLB).

A recent health study by Duke University has found that "hot-heads" frequently have poorer health. The studies found repeated anger to be as dangerous to the heart as smoking or high blood pressure.

Health is affected most in people who become angry at the little things. For example, they might blow up at a red traffic light or for dropping a quarter.

Anger is often a healthy emotion. We may get angry because people are starving, or because of war and death, or because we're being abused or seeing someone else abused. However, I believe you will find that most things aren't worth the effort. We only hurt ourselves by flying off the handle with every minor irritation.

You seem to do a good job at controlling your emotions. You will not be sorry that you mastered them instead of them mastering you.

Love,
Dad

Something to Think About:

1. Do you think Jesus got angry? If so, what made Him angry?
2. Is anger a problem for you? If so, list three ways to help overcome it.
3. Should you ever remain angry over something? Explain.

About Swearing

Dear June,

Have you heard some of the words that are being used on television? It seems to me that those words could be left unsaid without losing a single programming point. And it's not only the words they use but the subjects they discuss and the way they discuss them.

I won't attempt to list all the dirty words I've heard, nor will I try to divide them into categories. However, here are a few principles to keep in mind.

Don't say anything your parents don't want you to say. This is simply good sense, because an intelligent teenager does not use words which might get him into trouble—it's simply not worth getting grounded or sent to your room. You may think the word is harmless, but parents are the final authority on word control.

Ask your parents for an explanation. Try to do this when all of you are calm and in a good humor. You deserve an explanation and most parents will be happy to give one.

Cruel words are as bad as swearing. Neither are acceptable, of course, but the mean words we use to hurt others are as much of an attack on God as swearing. Calling someone "stupid" attacks his self-worth. "Fats," "creep" or "retardo" are terrible put-downs and a direct denial of the Golden Rule. Some people's self-esteem is weak all through life because they were called names when they were children.

Earthy words are ugly. Why do some feel they have to toss around bathroom words or worse? Is it because they want to shock people? Is it because they are angry? Is it because they want to be like others? Is it because they don't know very many words? No matter how hard we try, we won't find a good reason.

Don't throw God's name around. As a matter of respect we need to handle God's name with care. To merely throw it out carelessly, without meaning, is to show disrespect. The Bible tells us, "You shall not use the name of Jehovah your God irreverently" (Ex. 20:7, TLB).

Keep words in perspective. It's a little silly to sit around debating over which words are acceptable and which expressions are okay when there are more serious Christian questions. There are billions who have not heard of the love of Christ. There are millions who are starving to death. Those are the really significant Christian issues.

Love,
Dad

Something to Think About:

1. What do you think about swearing?
2. How will you train your children about swearing when you become a parent?
3. Do you know people who have formed a habit of swearing and can't seem to break it?
4. What does your family or church group think about words like "golly," "gee whiz" and "heck"?

How to Argue with Parents (and Not Get Grounded)

Dear June,

Parents aren't always right. It hurts me to say that, but it's true. I know, because I am a parent.

That must be one of the most frustrating parts of being a teenager—to realize at times that you are correct and yet unable to change the mind of a parent. But you will experience such situations many times as you grow older. It is only another of the roles you will have to fulfill in life. A lot of time will seem wasted trying to change the ideas of a teacher, a boss, an inspector or a spouse. You might be smart to gain a few skills in how to argue without getting into trouble. They are weapons in the war against stubborn giants.

Here are a few clues. You may add a couple of your own:

Never yell at a parent. It probably raises his blood pressure, blocks off his thinking process and makes his reflexes want to say no. A calm sentence is more likely to draw a calm response.

Never call a parent a name. Honorary titles like "Director," "Grouch," and "Old Man" are seldom welcomed. You can't get grounded for what you are thinking, but you can spend the evening in your room for what you say.

Know the facts. Nothing kills a discussion more quickly than a dull "I don't know." Collecting solid information will help both you and your parents make good decisions.

Clean your room. Teenagers never win arguments when their room is messy. Parents are not being shown you are a responsible person. By taking the responsibility of cleaning your room, you may gain your desired freedom in some other area. Never start an argument with a messy room or an unfinished chore. Parents always win there.

Never threaten a parent. Phrases like "I won't tell you where your Pat Boone tape is" will not work. "If you don't let me go, I'll hide your *National Geographic*" is another bummer. If you want your parents to hear your side of the argument, stick to the facts.

Always say "please" and "thank you." These two words will gain you pardon for a caveful of sins. It really burns adults when they see rude young people. Any clue that their child might be polite turns them into grateful putty.

These are merely helps. The best argument is to have a good cause in the first place. However, if you use these you will probably be going more places and getting to stay longer.

Love,
Dad

Something to Think About:

1. Have you ever thought your parents were illogical? How do you convince them about something new?
2. Do your parents stop listening when you try to convince them of something? If so, what can you do?
3. What works best with your parents when you are trying to change their minds?

When Are You an Adult?

Dear June,

A few years ago a New England senator voted against a bill that a former President of the United States wanted. To get even, the President made it harder for the senator to get special visitor passes to the White House.

I remember thinking it was a childish way to act. Doesn't it sound a great deal like holding your breath or kicking dirt on someone else's shoes?

The question of adulthood is confusing. Some adults do act childish, while some young people show tremendous responsibility.

We describe adults by using their legal age. But it's not the best description because some grown-ups behave so badly that they should be sent to their rooms or have their "toys" taken away. Haven't you thought so too?

Adulthood is an age because there are legal guidelines. However, real adulthood is reached by behavior. A person who doesn't do his job, who is rude, who hurts others, who can't keep his promises, who can't be on time, acts like a child regardless of his age or size.

Paul explained the transition:

"It's like this: when I was child I spoke and thought and reasoned as a child does. But when I became a man my thoughts grew far beyond those of my childhood, and now I have put away the childish things" (1 Cor. 13:11, TLB).

It may not work for everyone, but for most young people there are some simple ways to show parents you are growing up.

*You do your job without being told twice.
*You can tell time and avoid being late.

*You accept school work as your responsibility and get it done.

*You build trust. Your parents know they can believe what you say.

That sounds simple but they are important building blocks to becoming an adult. Few young people have proved they are adults by sitting angrily at the dinner table. And few teenagers have shown their maturity by coming home an hour late. No young person ever became an adult by insulting his parents.

You live in an area that's hard to define. You are not a child. That's obvious from your appearance and your conversation. You are not an adult yet; you have years of training and school to finish.

In that twilight zone the best you can do is act like an adult. That's the way people take you seriously. So far you are handling the twilight zone well.

Love,
Dad

Something to Think About:

1. Recently, have you been treated like a child? How did you feel?
2. In what way have you shown maturity in the last three months?
3. If a member of your family continues to treat you as a child, what should you do?

Saying, "I Love You"

Dear June,

Why are the most important words in life often difficult to say? For example, words like "please," "I'm sorry," "forgive me," or even "thank you." Sometimes they are bubbling up inside and want to flow over with sincerity but we may stop them from coming out.

Whatever makes them hard to say is probably the same reason why "I love you" often can catch in our throats. It's embarrassing because it may uncover our deepest emotions and we don't want to expose them. And sometimes we aren't sure how the words will sound, so we choke them back.

Many adults have trouble saying caring words to their children or young people. That is too bad, since all of us need to hear them. Caring words are like medicine which heals deep inside.

Even though "I love you" may sound awkward and stumble out rather than flow out when we say it, the words need to be said—and often. The more we say them the smoother it will sound and the gentler it will move.

If you aren't ready to say the words, you might want to leave a note. Something like "Thanks, Mom, for the new top" and then add, "Love, June." You should make it a normal way of expressing yourself.

Sometimes try to come up behind your mother, put your arms around her, thank her for something, and add "I love you." If you do this a few times, it might not be long before you can look her in the eye and say the same thing.

If this sounds too mushy now, you'll find before long it will seem normal. The amount of good you do yourself and your mother will be well worth any embarrassment in getting used to it.

Saying "I love you" is a mature way to address a loving relationship. There are many ways you can show love too. For example, giving a present, or helping around the house. However, everyone would like to hear the words from a warm, sincere voice.

Jesus had many ways to demonstrate His love. Yet He also appreciated the importance of verbalizing it. We don't know how often Jesus did this, but we do know He was willing to put "I love you" into words.

Say it to your parents—it makes them feel great.

"I have loved you even as the Father has loved me" (John 15:9, TLB).

Love,
Dad

Something to Think About:

1. What are some ways you have found to express your love?
2. To whom has it been hardest to say "I love you"?
3. Can you remember when someone said "I love you" and it meant a great deal? Explain.

Death Comes Hard

Dear Jim,

I think our society has become stiff and reserved to the point where it is hard to show emotions. For instance, if you are a guy and you face the fear of losing a job, the norm seems to be to hold your feelings in. That can leave many men without any way to express their emotions. It seems we are expected either to bottle up our feelings or swallow them.

How does someone react to death and still feel macho? We think we can't cry. And if you are a teenager, you aren't expected to send flowers. So how does a guy say "I love," "I care," "I hurt"?

When we stand beside a casket, as most of us will someday, we may want to cry. We might feel like letting it loose and being ourselves. However, so often we think that strong men don't cry. So we swallow hard, look away and then walk out of the room. If we cry, we cry alone.

What you did at your grandmother's funeral was a good way to express yourself. Without telling anyone, you slipped your track medal under the pillow in your grandmother's casket. It was personal, caring and sharing. The medal was buried with her. And you decided to not tell anyone until after the funeral.

Death is sad enough by itself. But it becomes much harder if we have no way to express our feelings. You found a way—your way—to say "I love you," "I will miss you." Like the woman who washed Jesus' feet with expensive perfume (Luke 7:45–47), you reached out in love.

You are smart to find avenues to express your feelings. And they are sincere and honest. When you

can let them out, you are helping yourself and
everyone else.

Love,
Dad

Something to Think About:

1. Has your best friend had a family death that made
   him very sad? What did you do to help him?
2. Have you faced a death of someone you loved?
   What helped you at that time?
3. How would you explain death to a child?

Nine Feet Tall

Dear June,

Congratulations! You reached out and you got it. I never dreamed that a famous singer would write back and personally sign the letter. It was not just a short letter either, but paragraphs of good helpful advice answering your questions.

I don't even know who Lionel Richie is, but he must be a thoughtful person. He knows how to make someone feel nine feet tall because he was kind and took time to reach out.

My guess is that this memory will hang high in your mind for many years. It was a good lesson in caring. So, whenever you get the chance to do someone a favor or drop him a thank you note, you might remember what this letter meant to you.

The meaning of life is not the big things. Often its best moments are in a handshake, a smile, a phone call, a letter. These will pick people up and make them feel great. And isn't that a part of the work of God? We need to be busy encouraging each other, helping each other to dream and daring others to hope.

Too many people feel defeated, run over and useless. Every chance you get, give them a shot in the arm and get them dreaming again.

When God sent His Son to earth for us, He showed us many good things like love and sacrifice. However, one of the strongest virtues He taught us was how to be kind.

"And now God can always point to us as examples of how very, very rich his kindness is, as shown in

all he has done for us through Jesus Christ" (Eph.
2:7, TLB).

> *Love,*
> *Dad*

Something to Think About:

1. What have you done for someone else that made
   him feel really good?
2. There are probably people to whom you are a hero.
   Can you think of some?
3. Can you think of ways Christ encouraged others?

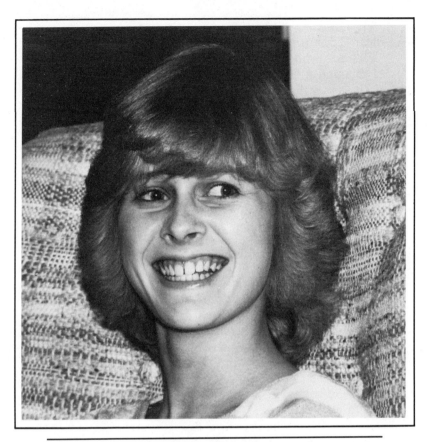

Live It Up

Dear June,

How many times have you been to a school play that everyone seemed to enjoy? I remember listening to people talk after a play and practically everyone was excited about the girl who had the lead. Angela was excellent, her face radiated and we sometimes forgot she was playing a part.

"Angela is easily the best actress in the school," one parent beamed as he walked past.

I shook my head in agreement, but inside my heart said no. Angela was the best actress on the stage that night. There was no doubt of that. However, I felt sure that the best actress was probably someone who didn't even try out, a teenager who sat in the audience who could have done an even better job. Yet, I imagine it was hard for that teenager to overcome her shyness and give it a try. Of course I didn't know who she was, but I was sure she was there.

Most of us seem to think of teenagers as a bold, boisterous group who talk a lot and will try anything. I think that is only one side of a young person. Often they also feel shy, self-conscious and awkward. There are many young people who want to try, who want to get involved, but their own shyness holds them back.

The great majority of youth has a certain amount of bashfulness. Their life is changing—their hair, body and voices *are all* in transition. Because of this, they become less sure of themselves.

Shyness is to be expected by most teens (but not by all) and frequently they grow out of its worst stages. However, half the population remains self-conscious and awkward. These people enter adulthood, jobs, and parenting, painfully shy.

Shyness is not only hurtful; it is also a terrible waste of the talents, gifts and abilities God has given us to enjoy and use.

"The Bible tells us, "Now God gives us many kinds of special abilities, but it is the same Holy Spirit who is the source of them all" (1 Cor. 12:4, TLB).

It is impossible to know if we can do something unless we try. However, we hold back to protect ourselves, making sure we don't get hurt. Yet, the greater hurt is that we were afraid to try.

You seem to have a good feeling of self-confidence. That quality can help to make a lot of your dreams come true. As you go through high school, keep that eagerness to give your abilities a try. Between God's gifts for you and your willingness to use them, you are bound to find life exciting.

Love,
Dad

Something to Think About:

1. How do you know the difference between showing off and doing something because you want to?
2. Is there something that is hard for you to try? Why? What can you do about it?
3. Is there something you do well but you don't want to let others know? Why?

The Great Zit Invasion

Dear June,

I don't think God created acne.

Don't ask me to prove that; it's merely a gut feeling. I don't believe God created warts, chicken pox or flat feet, either.

Acne is the result of a good body reaction; however, that doesn't mean the zit itself is good. I don't think there is a right age to get acne, but the teen years seem particularly affected. I know appearance is important and you are wondering how your features will finally turn out. And in an unsettled time of life, the last thing you need is a cheek full of pimples.

Unfortunately, some teenagers develop a shyness during the zit age and never fully come out of it. Even though this may seem like a hard period in your life, you will recover. Buy the creams or whatever helps to keep them in control and bide your time.

Zits are a bad deal and there is no sense in trying to say nice things about them. The Bible says, don't call bad things good (Prov. 17:15). Life is full of bad deals, but like others who have weathered through unhappy years, you will come out shining like a hubcap.

Love,
Dad

Something to Think About:

1. If your best friend is troubled with acne, could you give him some suggestions?
2. What are some other areas that trouble young people?
3. What permanent harm comes if a young person becomes overly shy at this stage of life?

Inviting Christ In

Dear Jim,

As you look around society you are seeing a wide
variety of religious experiences. Some people shave
their heads, stare at the sun or ring bells. Others
take drugs or chant all night long. Each of these
appear to be an attempt to find God and keep Him
happy. At best it sounds like tough work—trying to
cover over a guilty conscience. At worst it results in
very severe deception and bizarre actions.

With so much confusion you can be glad that God
sent His Son to forgive us of our sins. This was not
someone having another vision and new revelations.
This was the historical Christ whose life and death
were verified with facts. If His resurrection was not
historical and could not be trusted, you and I might
be eating bark or collecting barrels of earthworms
hoping that we might please God.

Guessing about God can't be much fun; in fact, it's
frightening. It's reassuring to know that God has
clearly shown us the way to salvation and to a clear
conscience concerning our sin. You can find peace
with God by agreeing with Him that you have
disobeyed what He has said, by confessing those sins,
and by inviting Jesus Christ into your life.
Immediately He forgives our sins and makes us
members of His family. It is simple but evidently God
didn't want to make it complicated.

To some people, the date they invited Jesus Christ
in is very significant. They write it in their Bibles
and tell others the day. For others, they can remember
the occasion but dates and locations are not
important. Still others cannot remember an exact
time but know that they have turned their lives over
to Christ.

Whichever may have been the case, it is good to know that the search for God is over, because He has found you. You are forgiven and have a definite place in heaven. You know Jesus Christ now as the Lord of every area of your life and He is in control!

Life will be filled with many surprises. Some of them will be terrible disappointments, others will be times of overwhelming happiness. Whatever life's curves have to offer, it is great to know that you have settled life's largest question. You have invited Jesus Christ to become your Savior from sin and Lord of your life. To know Him overshadows all that will ever come your way.

"Now we rejoice in our wonderful new relationship with God—all because of what our Lord Jesus Christ has done in dying for our sins—making us friends of God" (Rom. 5:11, TLB).

Love,
Dad

Something to Think About:

1. Do you ever talk with your family or friends about becoming a Christian?
2. If you know Christ, how has that helped you?
3. Do you know someone who has recently become a Christian? Explain.

The Self-esteem Problem

Dear June,

Everyone is talking about self-esteem, so it must be important. The subject is so popular that discussing it has almost become a trend. I hate to chase fads, but this one is worth discussing. I think the problem of self-esteem is one of the most serious of our time.

Many of the difficulties we face as adults are often the result of poor self-esteem as children. We are growing up in an unstable, highly competitive, rapidly changing society, and I believe we are suffering from it.

There is no magic wand to give a person healthy self-esteem. However, there are a few steps that could make it easier to establish. At least give these some thought.

Let people love you. You have a family who loves you deeply. We spend time with you, play games, go places, wrestle and talk together for hours. Don't resist the flow of love. Try to accept it and give it in return. Because throughout your life those experiences will remind you that you are lovable and capable of loving.

Find things you like to do. This is another one of your strong points. Your activities don't have to be the biggest or the best. However, it is important to know that you can do things.

Be a good friend. You are fortunate to have such excellent friends. A few deep, dependable friendships make you feel good about yourself.

Accept the total love of God. This is one of the hardest facts for some people to accept. We often see God as happy in the morning and angry by mid-afternoon. We may picture Him as an inconsistent

God who is likely to be angry with us at any moment.

If you see God that way, it's hard to feel settled and secure. God's love is constant, dependable and unchanging. He is your heavenly Father today, tomorrow and forever. His love for you is immovable. Read that sentence again.

Even when we do something dreadfully wrong, God reaches out His arms of forgiveness. That much you can count on.

"But God is so rich in mercy; he loved us so much" (Eph. 2:4, TLB).

You seem to be well on the road to feeling good about yourself. You are valuable, not because you make the team or score so many points, but because you are lovable and loving to others.

Love,
Dad

Something to Think About:

1. Do you know someone with low self-esteem? How could this be helped?
2. Name ten things you do well.
3. Name five people who love you.

Einstein Quit

Dear Jim,

Albert Einstein wasn't always a respected genius. When he was a teenager, Einstein was confused, disappointed and fairly aimless. After a dull career in school, he finally quit at the age of 15. He then drifted from one uneventful job to another and even tried school a few more times.

After years of fumbling around, Einstein sat down to write three papers. Those papers, written by a lackluster dropout, stunned the scientific world.

Stories like this can be repeated often about great people: famous inventors, successful businessmen, creative geniuses. They are the tales of people who did what they wanted to do and eventually saw their dreams come true.

These stories need to be repeated because so many young people get down on themselves. They don't seem to fit into the school scene and frequently begin to believe they are useless. This is most damaging because they soon stop dreaming. Consequently they take the first job that comes along instead of reaching out for what they really would like to do.

The world of opportunity remains open to you. Of course you can't do everything you want; none of us can. All of us do have limitations. However, those restrictions aren't as many as we might think.

Don't be afraid to dream. God has a way of making dreams come true. They might not happen without hard work, but they can become reality. Most of us are limited only by our ability to dream.

God is in the business of making dreams come true.

"If a child asks his father for a loaf of bread, will he be given a stone instead? If he asks for fish, will he be given a poisonous snake? Of course not! And if you hardhearted, sinful men know how to give gifts to your children, won't your Father in heaven even more certainly give good gifts to those who ask for them?" (Matt. 7:9–11, TLB).

Love,
Dad

Something to Think About:

1. Think of a dream you may have. How can you help it become reality?
2. Do you know someone who isn't a scholar who does well in other areas?
3. What area is your strongest—people, athletics, music, creativity, other?

Your Big Race

Dear June,

It wasn't exactly the race of the century, but it was exciting. The other girl had beaten you in the 1200 early in the year and later you had beaten her. And you were now looking forward to the rematch.

As the date of the race grew closer, you practiced harder. She had defeated you easily the first time, which was almost humiliating for you. You were determined this time. I hadn't realized how much it meant to you until you took yourself out of the other race. You did this so you could be fresh and give it everything you had.

Then the surprise came. The girl you wanted to beat took herself out of the other race, too. Both of you would be ready and possibly at your best.

When you lined up and the gun was shot, you jumped out into second place. You stayed there, just ahead of the girl you wanted to beat, until the second lap when you took the lead. In the third lap you may have tired some. As you came into the final stretch, the other girl poured it on and she won the race by one-tenth of a second.

In a little over four minutes you learned so much about living. You realized you can't always win, even if you prepare your very best. You also discovered there was happiness in losing even when you gave it your all. It was a wonderful lesson and a second place you could be proud of.

Most importantly, your loss did not make you bitter. You shook the hand of the girl who won, and when you walked over to see us you didn't say one thing about her. This showed us you were a good sport.

Maybe next year you will meet that girl again and

you will come up the winner—and then maybe not. Possibly you will never beat her. But that would be all right, too. You will continue to learn by participating. What you learn by winning and by losing made the race well worth running.

I think the rest of your life will be like a race. You will win some and lose some. And the thrill of it will be in learning either way.

Most important is that you do participate. You should reach out, stretch and endure the pain to obtain the goals that you set and God makes available to you.

Far back in your race was a girl who never had a chance. She had dropped back at the beginning and soon most people forgot she was running. Long after the cheering was over she finished last. Without praise, without hope, without fanfare, she finally crossed the line. But she also won. She had finished the race set before her.

The Bible also tells us of a race. "I strain to reach the end of the race and receive the prize for which God is calling us up to heaven because of what Christ Jesus did for us" (Phil. 3:14, TLB).

Love,
Dad

Something to Think About:

1. Is competition overemphasized in your school? If so, what can you do about it?
2. If sports are overemphasized in your life, what can be done to remedy this?
3. If someone is not a good athlete, what can be done to give him strong self-esteem?

Getting Behind

Dear Jim,

It's no fun running track if you're always behind. There isn't much drive during practice if you think you can't win anyway. I think you would get discouraged and possibly give up.

That same despair sets in when you begin to get behind in school. You may discover that the enthusiasm of the first weeks doesn't last. Soon you begin to slide backwards. And before long you look for excuses to skip school. The person who keeps getting behind usually becomes miserable. He doesn't know what is being discussed in class. Consequently he lives in fear of being called on. Sometimes he turns to jokes, hoping to cover up what he doesn't know.

If he isn't careful, this person will get down on himself and begin to think he is stupid. For him, the problem is one of being lost. He has failed to keep up and before long he feels hopeless. And now he's so far behind he feels buried under unfinished chapters and unwritten papers. From that position, he has little hope of winning.

It's hard to do schoolwork on a steady, daily basis. To do so there has to be self-discipline, a desire to keep up and a good feeling about yourself. A feeling that if you plug away—every day—you can make it and make it well.

I feel sorry for people who get hopelessly behind. It is the feeling of quiet terror.

If you keep up every day, school becomes manageable. That gives you the feeling of accomplishment and self-confidence.

Do yourself a favor. Make yourself a pledge. This is the year you want to do your work on a daily basis.

"A little extra sleep, a little more slumber, a little

folding of the hands to rest means that poverty will break in upon you suddenly like a robber, and violently like a bandit" (Prov. 24:33, 34, TLB).

Love,
Dad

Something to Think About:

1. Have you ever been behind in a class? What was it like?
2. List some guidelines to help someone keep up with daily classwork and homework.
3. How can you encourage someone who has difficulty in school?

Getting Along with Teachers

Dear June,

If I asked you what you study in school, your reply would probably be a list of subjects. That is the usual answer, but I disagree. I would say most of a student's time is spent studying teachers. They are the center of education.

It is from teachers that we learn whether or not a subject is interesting. They pass enthusiasm or dullness to us. They also teach us how they handle authority. Some are bossy because I'm sure they never learned what good leadership quality is. Others have a positive, fair attitude and we willingly work for them.

A student recently said, "You can tell the difference between Mr. Brown and Mr. Green. When you do something wrong, Mr. Brown corrects your mistake. With Mr. Green, it's different; he attacks you personally." Some teachers have much to learn themselves.

Teenagers watch, they understand and they know what is happening. Hopefully they are picking out the good qualities they see and will cultivate these for themselves.

How many teachers can you think of who are pleasant, helpful and willing to lead? There are many of them and they make up for the few who seem unhappy in their jobs. The writer of Proverbs says it is the pleasant teacher who is the best (Prov. 16:21).

Some people believe the best teachers are the gruff, insulting, nasty ones. Do you really think that is true? I never bought it. A teacher can show discipline, set high standards, and insist on good performance without becoming the school grouch.

I didn't write this to pick on teachers. I certainly

didn't write to pick on you. You seem to get along well with them. However, I would like to make a few suggestions for you to consider.

First, if you ever get a difficult teacher, remember that you have something to offer. When you react with pleasantness, you are more likely to change the teacher's mood. Don't let a grump turn you into a grump.

Second, learn how to get along with grouchy people; you will have to do it the rest of your life. You may find Mr. Grouch in the store, on the job, on the track or in the church. If Mr. Grouch can ruin your day, you are in for a lot of bad days.

Third, you do a good job of keeping your balance whatever the teacher's personality. And whenever you get a chance to teach, remember to be firm, fair and pleasant.

Love,
Dad

Something to Think About:

1. Describe the best teacher you ever had.
2. Would you like to be a teacher? Why?
3. If you were addressing the Teachers Association in your town, what would you tell them about how to be a better teacher?
4. Remember to pray for *all* your teachers.

Household Jobs

Dear Jim,

Which job do you dislike the most? You don't seem to mind mowing the lawn or painting. My well-educated guess is that the inside jobs are the ones that irritate you the most. Doing the dishes once a week, cleaning the bathroom once a month and having to wash your own clothes are the ones that you complain about.

I think the reason is that you associate them with girls' jobs. That has always been a killer. Boys don't want to be called girls or have anything to do with their activities. Why I don't know.

How did jobs become divided into categories? It's as if cars belong to men and cooking belongs to women. Who set those rules? Who drew those boundaries? God didn't say that people who sew are sissies. He didn't say that carpenters had to be men.

Those distinctions fall quickly when it comes to a family living together in a house. Some families learn how to share jobs because they want and need to be kind to each other. For instance, we all use and want a clean bathroom. And we all need clean dishes. So everyone should pitch in and do his part in helping.

Some of the best cooks are men. Some of the best athletes are women. One of the best drag racers in the world is a woman. There shouldn't be neat little roles that men and women must follow.

The role of helping spreads into both genders. That's why it is all right for a boy to vacuum. It's just as reasonable for a girl to scrape paint.

Thanks for taking care of your jobs. You grumble some, but that's okay. You still usually get things done. That means we are family pulling together. It

feels good to belong to a group that helps each other—
even when we don't always like doing it.

"Be kind to each other" (Eph. 4:32, TLB).

Love,
Dad

Something to Think About:

1. What kinds of jobs would you assign teenagers if you were a parent?
2. Do you feel you've been overworked? Not worked enough?
3. Do you ever volunteer to help a family member who has much to do?

No Longer a Kid

Dear Jim,

Getting a driver's license is a gigantic leap in our society. One day you are chauffeured around like a carton of eggs in danger of cracking. Then it seems soon afterward you are in total control of tons of steel and screeching rubber. When you take the driver's seat, you're in charge of a powerful machine. You also hold the keys to greater freedom than you have ever known.

Once you have tasted that much independence, it is hard to ever see yourself as a child again. Could you see yourself following your parents around and riding on playground equipment? No, children don't have keys jangling from their pocket and sunglasses twirling from their hand. Children don't go alone for shakes at the drive-in or play music at top volume. Driving is a new world and you are part of it.

You will never be a child again. Even though someone might call you a "kid," or refer to you as one of our children, you realize you're moving into the "young adult" world. You are too old and too independent to ever be a child again. Even though you are largely dependent and under the control of your parents, no one can send you back into the small world of children again.

Now that we have settled your classification, we move to the next question. How mature will you choose to be as a young adult? You seem to be enjoying the young adult life now. Generally you handle your life well. When a job needs to be done, or you have to be some place on time, you're dependable.

I hope you continue to mature as a young adult. There is really no other place for you to go. You are too big and too old to fit back into the life of a child.

It is gone forever. You can't go back. Neither can you drag your childhood into the young adult world. You cannot continue to act like a 12-year-old.

You have crossed the threshold into the world of adults. I think you will get along well there because you are eager to act maturely. You are growing up well.

"It's like this: when I was a child I spoke and thought and reasoned as a child does. But when I became a man my thoughts grew far beyond those of my childhood, and now I put away the childish things" (1 Cor. 13:11, TLB).

Love,
Dad

Something to Think About:

1. How do you handle who puts gas in the car?
2. How do you handle chores at your house?
3. Have your parents given you enough freedom? Give suggestions.

Test Your Maturity

Dear June,

I've decided people seem to be running in the wrong direction. Adults buy cosmetics, wear clothing and drive cars that will make them look younger. Teenagers are buying cosmetics, wearing clothing and driving cars to make them look older. What a goofy lot we are.

I guess this does tell us that in order to know who is a mature person, we need to do more than look at them. And like most of your friends, you would like to prove that you are grown up.

There are several tests you can take which prove maturity to me. Like pills, they are each unpleasant and difficult to swallow. Nevertheless, give them a try.

Test number one: *Can you tell time?*

Mature people arrive where they are supposed to on time. They thought their plans through. First, they knew how much time they needed to get ready. And second, they knew how long a time it would take to get there. Less mature types are frequently half an hour to an hour late, complete with a list of odd excuses.

Test number two: *Can you handle responsibility?*

That means a person will get the job done when he is told to do it. He will put some personal activity aside so the job will be done on time. Immature types always have things half done or they pretend to forget to do them at all.

Test number three: *Do you take initiative?*

If you see something that needs to be picked up, put back, turned off, opened or closed, do you do it without being told? The favorite saying of the immature is "It wasn't my job."

Test number four: *Are you thankful?*

A baby grabs things and puts them into his mouth. As he grows older he grabs things, looks them over and then puts them into his mouth. When he becomes mature, he politely accepts things, says thank you and then puts them into his mouth.

The person who perpetually complains, who sees no good, who is grateful for little or nothing, is immature, no matter what his age. You could give him the world and he would still grump.

I believe I could see the day your sister grew up. Suddenly, like a storm, she began telling people "thank you," because she had become a truly grateful person. Paul put it crisply, "And always be thankful" (Col. 3:15, TLB).

You do well at these. I hope you keep these helpful guidelines in mind as you continue your race into maturity.

Love,
Dad

Something to Think About:

1. What are some things young people do that show immaturity?
2. List some things you do that show maturity.
3. If your friends are acting immature and want you to go along, what do you do?

Respect for the Car

Dear Jim,

We appreciate the respect you show for the family car. I do have some simple rules for you to keep in mind. They help me relax when you are borrowing the car. You do most of these well—most of the time.

1. Always ask to borrow the car.

It's frustrating to be ready to go out with your mother only to find you have taken the good car and left us the green bomb. The green bomb doesn't have air conditioning and should never be driven out of town without notifying the rescue squad. We feel much better knowing you would not take the car (even for a few minutes) without checking.

2. Pick up the pop bottles.

You basically have neat friends but sometimes they forget. So, please clean out the car when you're done driving. It's a miserable feeling to slide into the car and sit in the middle of a pile of someone else's trash—especially if some of that trash leaves chocolate on your good clothes. It also bugs us to drive off in a hurry and have three bottles roll out from under the seat and rock back and forth all the way to our destination. I'm not complaining, of course.

3. Put gas in the car.

We know you aren't rich, but then we aren't either. So my heart warms over like a waffle when I see the gas gauge is up. You do that quite a few times without saying anything. Thanks.

4. Have respect for yourself, others, and the law.

If this seems harmless to some, I take it seriously (as you know). It isn't simply a question of whether or not you can afford to pay for the ticket if you have been caught speeding. The real question is respect. We need to know you have respect for yourself, your passengers, the car, the police and the law. Disregard for any of these shows disrespect.

Many people may get tickets. But, none of us can afford to show disrespect if we choose to drive a car.

Thanks for being a good driver. We don't sit at home wondering if you are being careful. We appreciate the thoughtfulness you show.

Love,
Dad

Something to Think About:

1. If you have gotten a traffic ticket, how did your parents react?
2. What are some guidelines you would make for a family who shares a car or cars?
3. When should you be allowed to have your own car? Who will pay for it? Who will pay for upkeep?

The Drug Dropout

Dear June,

It's important to find some good escapes in your
life. If you don't, the pressures can become too much.
That's why people have hobbies, play ball or go
cruising. I think you can see that already in high
school. The daily work load gets to all of us
sometimes.

The sad fact is that many young people are not
finding the good escapes—from peer pressure, school
pressure, family tension, or dissatisfaction with
themselves. Consequently, when the pressure gets to
them, they turn to drugs. Record numbers of teenagers
are finding their escape in drugs. Unfortunately many
have trouble finding their way back again.

The problem has become so serious in Los Angeles
that the police estimate that 60% of the high school
seniors use drugs two or three times a week. They
believe that on a given school day one-fourth of the
seniors are stoned. By the time they graduate, 80% of
the class will have tried drugs at least once.

The statistics are merely numbers until you hear
of someone who smashed a car, flunked out of school
or robbed a store while using drugs. Then you see
them as individuals messing up their lives because
they didn't learn to be happy with some safe escapes.

Other studies asked what kind of youth is more
likely to turn to drugs. Frequently, but not always, it
was the teenager who had poor relationships with
his parents. For a girl, it was often a poor
relationship with her father.

Family relationships are complex. Parents and
young people need to know that they care for each
other. Not merely that they are physically related, but
that they are emotionally attached. When one hurts,

the other is affected. When one is happy, that feeling spills over to the other.

That doesn't mean that the young people who use drugs must have bad parents. Young people make their own decisions. However, those who have good relationships have a better chance of staying away from drugs.

That is only one of the reasons why it is important for us to keep talking, keep playing games and going out for Cokes. Those times make me stronger and I think they make you stronger, too.

I read of a loving father named Jairus who pushed through the crowds to see Jesus because his daughter was dying. Jairus must have loved his girl greatly (Luke 8:41, 42). She was bound to feel that kind of love.

Love,
Dad

Something to Think About:

1. What are some good avenues of escape?
2. Are alcohol or drugs used heavily in your community? Explain.
3. What effect does your circle of friends have on you—for good or bad?

Do You Need a Curfew?

Dear Jim,

Right now one of the most important questions in the world is how late can you stay out at night. Inflation, space exploration and nuclear war all come in a poor second behind this big one.

The problem is just as perplexing for your parents as it is for you. What's fair? What's reasonable in a modern world? How much rope is too much for a teenager to handle?

To make the situation more complicated, your mother and I don't always agree. We try not to contradict each other, but we don't always lean the same way.

There is a lot to weigh in making the decision and a great deal to rule out. We can't go by your size— you are taller than either of us. We can't go by your age—some 16-year-olds have it together while others are strictly spaghetti.

To simply treat you like we do your sisters isn't fair. Everybody is an individual with his own set of strengths or weaknesses. I think those who put everyone into a pile called "teenagers" are making a serious mistake.

There are several guidelines that help parents understand the maturity of their teenagers. Fortunately, these are traits you handle well.

The first is *dependability*. When a teenager is on time, he is showing his parents that he can be responsible. That may sound like a funny gauge to use, but adults put great stock in it. If a young person can tell time and show up when he is expected, parents are delighted. We worry less and relax more. Our blood pressure drops and our stomachs grind less.

If someone is constantly 20 or 30 minutes late, his parents develop heartburn. Adult heartburn is bad for teenagers.

The second is *polite conversation.* When a teenager sounds demanding and insulting, he is automatically asking his parents to be negative.

Stomping out of the room, barking rude comments and endless pleas of how bad a teenager has it is self-centered and childish. This type of behavior makes a parent less than receptive. The parent may become determined to "teach the kid a lesson." We call that kind of communication "counter-productive."

It's a hard pill to swallow when a parent won't let you stay out late. Usually the best solution is to show you can handle the time they give you. It gives them vivid pictures of a teenager who is growing up.

Freedoms don't come as quickly as you might like, but there's hope. Your world is widening rapidly because you are maturing quickly.

You have been doing well at getting home on time. I think it shows you can be responsible.

Love,
Dad

Something to Think About:

1. Have your parents been more strict than parents of your friends? What rule would you change?
2. Why have your parents set coming-home times?
3. Do you show maturity by keeping commitments, being on time, completing assignments?

Treat Trust Carefully

Dear June,

There was a boy in our school named Ron who would rather lie than eat. Lying had become such a factor in his life that he found it hard to tell the truth about anything.

If someone asked what he did last night, Ron would lie about it, even when he had nothing to gain. It was almost as if he were afraid of the truth.

A lie sounds like an act. We speak of a lie as if it was something we do and it's over. A lie is far more; it is a destruction of trust. If a person is willing to lie, how do we know when he is telling the truth?

It is hard to relax with a liar, because we are on guard with our conversation. We hear what he says, but we don't know what he means.

Make yourself a valuable promise: You will never lie. Especially don't lie to your parents, because lying to them is particularly destructive. If they learn to distrust you, they become suspicious of other things you tell them and they will let you do fewer things. Lying will hurt you and everyone else it touches.

Your parents owe you the same promise. We must never lie to you. Whatever feelings you might develop about your parents, one solid block should remain: They will not lie to you.

Recently the newspaper printed some statistics on how many college students cheat in school. It suggested that there are a large number of people we cannot trust. If they get into a spot, they might find a dishonest way to get out of it.

So whether it is friendship, marriage, business, neighbors or parents, few things will hurt a relationship more than a lie. Know that parents are more open in allowing privileges if they know their teenager will not lie.

Thanks for building trust.

"Don't tell lies to each other" (Col. 3:9, TLB).

Love,
Dad

Something to Think About:

1. Do you know students at school who are not trusted by their teachers? Why?
2. Describe what you think is God's attitude toward lying.
3. Make every effort to adopt this motto: "No matter how hard it may be, I will always be honest with my parents."

The Horror Movie

Dear June,

You wish you had never seen it. Usually you know
when to turn off a TV show, but not always. When
we went to the cabin last weekend, I could see what a
horror show had done to you.

As soon as you saw a hatchet on the refrigerator
in the cabin, you took it into your bedroom and placed
it in the drawer. Only then did I remember that you
had seen a show about a hatchet murderer who
terrorized a camp.

After that you insisted on sleeping with your
sister. And several times you checked to make sure
the hatchet was still in the drawer.

More of us are haunted by fears than we would
like to admit. I grew up afraid of a werewolf. It was
the ugliest, meanest thing I had ever seen on the
movie screen. Your mother acquired a high fear of
snakes partly because she felt trapped by one when
she was five years old.

We all grow up with fears. Some of them are real
and unavoidable. But others we pick up by doing
dumb things.

Some teenagers and preteens seem to have a bent
toward horror shows. It's almost as if they want to
prove they are not afraid, when often they really are.
They will stay up to watch a show where a lady is
killed in the shower. That may sound harmless
enough; however, then they think about it every time
they take a shower—for years afterward. We must
be a little nuts to look for that kind of agony.

It probably doesn't do much good to tell young
people to stay away from shows like that. Horror
films are popular on television, in theaters and on
rental from the library.

116

Maybe the craze to watch horror movies could be compared to smoking, drugs or driving recklessly. Some of us think we need to live close to the edge of danger. Possibly we think we can chase fear away by rubbing shoulders with it. Too often this yen for danger backfires. It can ruin a vacation, make a shower an uneasy experience, or turn an evening walk into a nervous adventure.

The real fears of life are bad enough. Robberies, accidents, bankruptcies, divorce are real tragedies that do happen. What do we gain by collecting imaginary fears to make us miserable? Nothing.

It's your life and you have hard choices to make. I think the hatchet at the cabin will make some of your future choices easier.

"For I cried to him and he answered me! He freed me from all my fears" (Ps. 34:4, TLB).

Love,
Dad

Something to Think About:

1. What are some guidelines you would set for your children for watching TV?
2. How can you help overcome a deep fear? Give an example.
3. What are the pros and cons of horror shows?

The Music You Play

Dear June,

Some of the music I hear today is truly marvelous. It not only sounds great, but the lyrics are often first class. However, a few of the songs sound to me like broken garbage disposals. But there have always been differing opinions and tastes concerning music— even Wesley was criticized for using "pop" tunes for some of his hymns!

There is probably more about music that I do *not* understand than I do, so let me start here.

I don't understand why some of it has to be played so loudly. When it vibrates the car, my poor brain rattles and I develop a headache. I think it's difficult to enjoy music that leaves one visibly shaken. The medical concern about eardrum damage is not merely adult spoil-sports on the rampage again! Evidence shows that young people are actually doing permanent injury to their hearing by continually turning the volume too high on their stereos.

On the other hand, I don't understand why some

people attack the words, the performers and the beat of pop music so vigorously. Though I have heard horrendous stories about the personal lives of some rock stars and would guess that some of those are true, there surely are as spicy stories about lawyers, dentists, auto mechanics and bus drivers. It seems like we are clouding the issue. Immoral behavior should be rejected on any level. The personal lives of the musicians do not necessarily make the music itself bad.

If there are some things I don't understand, there are a few things I do.

I understand that young people are going to be attracted to music different from that of their parents. It is a matter of personal taste and maybe a statement of independence. Wouldn't that seem to be healthy and normal?

Further, I understand that most likely you will not appreciate the music of your own children and vice versa. This area of difference is part of the generation gap. We parents no doubt will sometimes ruefully shake our heads over your music—at least the volume—but I think we can come to a mutually satisfactory truce if we feel you are considering the possibility that music can have a profound effect on our moods and feelings. Thoughtful music can stretch our imagination; happy music can create a smile; and depressing music can be a real downer. Both music and words are saying something to you. Do they make you glad to be alive, glad to be a Christian? There is a place for sad music, but does it make you feel hopeless?

Being aware is a large part of enjoying music. Don't let it take your mind where you do not want it to go. The early Christians put a lot of emphasis on music.

"Talk with each other much about the Lord, quoting psalms and hymns and singing sacred songs, making music in your hearts to the Lord" (Eph. 5:19, TLB).

Love,
Dad

Something to Think About:

1. What kind of music do you like? What affect does it have on you?
2. What kind of Christian music do you like?
3. Do you like the music program at your school? the music used in your church? Why or why not?

Having Idols

Dear June,

It's fun to be a fan, isn't it? Whether it's sports or music, most of us like to have a special person we admire. We like someone who is exceptionally good at what he does. And often we find ourselves cheering for him to do even better.

All of us need heroes, even if they last but a short time. A hero has a way of lifting us up and making us feel great about life. When he has that effect on us, he can't be all bad.

Most of our heroes are shooting stars. By that I mean they might be television characters who rise up one season and are gone in a year or two. Your sister used to think the Hardy Boys were "hunks." She also liked the "Bee Gees" and Rick Springfield. With you it has been Lionel Richie and before that it was O. J. Simpson.

Adults can do the same thing. Some of them become enthused over political leaders, singers or good athletes. For myself, I've found a few great thinkers whom I appreciate.

Generally speaking, these "stars," "heroes" or "leaders" are good for us. They allow us to appreciate someone else who does things well, inspires us, and may even bring out the best in us.

The real harm seems to come when any of us puts too much faith in people. They are fragile at best and sometimes morally corrupt. You should learn what can and cannot be given to other people. (1) You can give someone your admiration but never your morals. (2) You can give someone your respect but never blind allegiance. (3) You can give them your attention but never a monopoly of your life.

People are fascinating, but if they become an obsession, they can hurt you.

In the age of posters all sorts of characters show up on the walls of teenagers' rooms. Many of them seem like decent people; a few look like escapees from chicken ranches.

They may have their place as long as they are a passing interest and their characters do not control us. When they begin to change our minds and our morals, or when we begin to surrender our judgment to theirs, they become idols. Idols in that sense are always wrong.

You are intelligent enough to know how much your heroes affect you. Occasionally try asking yourself some serious questions.

How does your hero affect your life?

Do you find yourself neglecting things you need to do?

Are you beginning to develop habits that you really are not proud of?

Do your heroes change or are you becoming too deeply engrossed with one?

Idols can come from the secular world or the religious world. Either way they can begin to block our view of Christ and become too powerful.

"So, dear friends, carefully avoid idol-worship of every kind" (1 Cor. 10:14, TLB).

Love,
Dad

Something to Think About:

1. Have you had a hero who disappointed you? Explain.
2. What characteristics of Jesus make Him a good hero?
3. Does someone look up to you as a hero?

Teenage Sex

Dear June,

Recently I heard a startling statistic. A professor claims that if a teenage girl becomes a mother and keeps her child, 87% of her major choices in life have already been made for her. Most of her boundaries are set and will not move.

But, despite that possibility, teenagers continue to have sex before they get married and millions regret it, often for the rest of their lives.

With so much awareness of sex today, you might imagine that the world is educated in this area. However, that doesn't seem to be the case. Many young people do not know the basic facts about how babies are made. They may have a general idea, but they would flunk a test on the particulars. And millions are flunking that test every year. The number of babies born to teenage mothers who were not married has doubled in the past ten years.

I think there are two main reasons why young people know so few facts about sex. First, and primarily, it is because adults do not feel comfortable talking about it. As adults we are often uptight concerning our own sexuality. The second reason is because young people want to pretend they know the facts when they may not. They may be afraid that they will look stupid to their "knowledgeable" peers. Actually, those peers may not know the facts either.

Consequently, young people are trapped. They feel a need to be sexually active without waiting until marriage. Movies, books and television seem to imply that "everyone is doing it." Therefore, they too frequently launch into a sexual relationship and they don't know what they are doing.

Secular society says that giving young people the

facts about the dangers of premarital sex doesn't work. That may be true for some. But I would like to think that there are teenagers who will use their heads instead of their glands.

There is just too much to lose in premarital sex. (1) You may give up a chance for a deeper, lasting love. (2) Your personal future could be jeopardized or greatly restricted. (3) If a pregnancy occurs, there is the happiness of the child to consider. (4) There are too many tears, broken hearts and too much guilt involved with premarital sex.

The warning issued in the Bible is a great help in removing any question about this: "But sexual sin is never right" (1 Cor. 6:13, TLB). This isn't God's attempt to deny us fun, love, and excitement. Rather, it's a control set to give us greater fun, greater love, greater excitement and real freedom. Do you know why? Because the best sex is *responsible* sex.

Many of us operate to a large extent on our emotions. Sometimes it's a great way to react. However, many teenagers are smart enough to use their brains. The ones who use their brains and their wills to say no have the least to cry over.

Love,
Dad

Something to Think About:

1. What are some situations to avoid because they create sexual temptations?
2. List some wholesome activities with which to fill spare time.
3. What effect does your particular group of friends have on you—for good or bad?

Normal Tension

Dear Jim,

Now that your body has become sexually mature, you are bound to face a lot of normal tension. Don't let that surprise you. The majority of teenage boys find the changes in their bodies confusing, sometimes embarrassing and occasionally frightening. If you can remind yourself of a few facts, you might find this stage of life a little easier to accept.

First, if you think about sex a great deal, don't panic. The amount of time differs among boys, but the average teenager has sex on his mind rather often. You aren't becoming a sex fiend or a pervert. Neither are you in danger of losing your mind.

Second, sex is one of our strongest drives. God made us that way so we would have a great desire to reproduce. The fact that you get the drive so early may be unfortunate, but it's certainly normal.

Third, by your developing other interests and avoiding situations that are too tempting, you can help yourself keep your sex drive in control. It's going to be hard to wait until you are married, but it is possible. It helps if you stay busy.

Fourth, teenagers are quite likely to have some fairly wild sexual fantasies. They might start soon after your body becomes sexually active. You should neither panic nor cultivate them. It's foolish to encourage fantasies, and they won't help you resist temptation.

Sometimes sexual fantasies appear in dreams. This happens to many teenagers and it's part of life. Some young people don't understand that and begin to think it only happens to them.

You will be better off if you know what is going on and know how to respond. The sex drive is a

powerful force and has a great influence on you.

When your sex drive is exercised in a marriage relationship, it can be an excellent gift from God. It is frequently hard to wait, but it is not impossible. You can do it!

"Let your manhood be a blessing; rejoice in the wife of your youth" (Prov. 5:18, TLB).

Love,
Dad

Something to Think About:

1. Do you have anyone to talk to or good resource books to answer questions you have about sex? Where could you go for information?
2. Do you know teenagers who don't know how to handle their sex drive and are getting themselves and others messed up?
3. What influence does your group of friends have on your standards?

New Feelings

Dear June,

Your body has left the world of the child and has started across the bridge into adulthood. The trip across is exhilarating, confusing, magnificent and a little frightening.

I can't pretend to know how a girl feels, but some experiences must be common to everyone. There must be some feelings of pride. You are no longer a child, because you have entered the realm of womanhood. Your body confirms that for you. As boys develop muscles and create whiskers, a girl's form also begins to change.

As your body changes, try to keep two facts in mind. Number one, a good figure has never made a girl a woman. You will become a woman by your behavior and character. Without character you would become only a fool in a woman's body. An insane secular society emphasizes body over character.

Number two, the person who must show off her body to get attention shows great immaturity. She proves she does not understand the importance of her character. If you have to show off your body to collect friends, you can be sure your values are confused.

The developing body of a woman opens the doors to sexual desire. That's a happy and normal fact. So don't feel guilty about it. Those are good, healthy feelings, and most of your friends share them. If they don't, they soon will. Too many young people think themselves evil because they have sexual desires. Not true.

However, sexual desire puts you in a dilemma, because it will be years before you can get married and carry out those desires. Consequently, you may face considerable frustration.

It would be smart if you would not feed those desires by putting yourself in tough situations. It is one thing to spend time with boys. But it is another to get yourself in predicaments where the sexual desire of each of you might become overpowering. By avoiding dark rooms, parked cars, back rows, and similar high-risk places, the easier it will be for you.

I know it's hard to hold your desires in check in a sex-crazy society. But don't make it harder by seeing how close you can get to danger.

Sex is great, but it's for marriage. I suggest you treat it like a good car. To do this, you keep a firm grip on the controls.

The writer of Proverbs warned his son this way, "Don't let your desires get out of hand" (7:25, TLB).

Love,
Dad

Something to Think About:

1. Do you know teenagers who use their bodies to get attention? What is your opinion of them?
2. What can families do to help this stage of growing up? Activities? Discussions? Other ideas?
3. Is your church doing a good job of planning activities for its young people? Explain.

When Death Passes By

Dear June,

Teenagers are full of life, energy, fun and hope. However, they are also serious thinkers who do not miss the deep emotions that surround them. Death is one of those heavy events that young people cannot ignore.

Your life has already been touched with death by the passing of your grandmother. Most teenagers have rubbed shoulders with it in some form or another. For instance, a few years ago in our town some high school students were killed in an accident. And three months ago a young mother died at age 32. Here and there a neighbor dies and leaves a gap.

Death will always be an uneasy visitor. On the one hand, death is evil. It destroys life, wrecks homes, leaves orphans, creates poverty, breaks hearts and gives birth to loneliness. Death is cruel because it separates and hurts. When you stand beside the coffin of a young mother, a child or a teenager, you will especially feel how much death tears your heart open.

On the other hand, death also has a way of becoming a friend. Death is the doorway to a new world, and becomes the passage into a life greater than any we could imagine. It is a place of activity, singing and sharing. It is a place that has been especially prepared by God and paid for by Jesus Christ.

Knowing that does not necessarily remove the pain of death. It still hurts. That's why many grown men cry at funerals. Because it is terrible to become separated from someone you care about so much.

Death can be a mixture of pain and hope, giving you a smashed heart, yet a feeling of peace.

When your grandmother died, you could see a wide

range of emotions. Some were quiet and chose to cry inside. Others wept openly. A few were cheerful and tried to think of the good side. Then others stayed busy and looked for practical ways to say they cared.

All of them were good ways to face death. Each felt and expressed his feelings in his own way.

If you live to a ripe old age, death will steal from you many times. Death will always be unkind and always be a doorway.

The more you talk about death the easier it is to face. Those who fear it the most are usually the ones who hurt the most.

How you react to death is a personal choice. Try to be natural and feel free to express yourself.

The good news in all of this is that eventually there will be no more death. God will destroy death.

"And there shall be no more death" (Rev. 21:4, TLB).

Love,
Dad

Something to Think About:

1. Have you had a close friend or family member die? What helped you most when you were hurting?
2. What is the hardest part about having someone die?
3. What difference does it make in your feelings if you believe in heaven?

What's Wrong with This World?

Dear June,

Teenagers have a rising awareness about injustices in our society. They realize that unfairness, even cruelty, does exist in our nation. This awareness is a good sign. We should be unhappy when people are treated badly and we need to take steps to correct this injustice.

Life is so much more than selecting the right jeans. It has more challenges than being seen with the right people. God expressed it this way:

"Tell them to be honest and fair—and not to take bribes—and to be merciful and kind to everyone. Tell them to stop oppressing widows and orphans, foreigners and poor people, and to stop plotting evil against each other" (Zech. 7:8–10, TLB).

There are terrible injustices. You have already been involved in correcting several. One was the Laotian family that needed someone to help them. They should not be left in a refugee camp. Unfortunately, their grandmother had already died there.

It was risky to become involved. What would they be like? Could we afford it? What if they couldn't get jobs? What if the community didn't like them? But we stuck in there and today they are well-established and doing excellently. Both parents accepted hard jobs and the children are in school. I believe they will soon be looking for their own home.

That was only one possibility. Remember the day you picked up debris from a farmer's field after the tornado? The coats, the clothes, the cash you gave to the family who needed them?

As you grow older, it would be wise not to forget those who suffer. Helping is close to the heart of God.

In this imperfect world we will not lack for opportunities to give assistance. Here are a few you might want to keep in mind:

*Young children who are falling behind in school and need a free tutor.

*Pregnant women who do not want an abortion but feel they have no alternative.

*People who could be helped tremendously by being taught to budget.

*The elderly who have chosen to live at home but need someone to run simple errands.

This is only a sample. One person can make a difference. Thanks for contributing.

Love,
Dad

Something to Think About:

1. Name an injustice you are aware of. What could you do about it?
2. Have you ever been treated unjustly? Explain.
3. Why does God allow injustice to take place?

The Uncertain Future

Dear Jim,

Last year I led a discussion group in Canada and I asked what kind of pressure young people might be facing. One person offered this suggestion, "With so much talk about nuclear war and about the return of Christ, even Christian kids feel there is no tomorrow so get the most you can today."

Both of the events are real possibilities. The return of Christ would be a welcomed interruption into the world. However, the events described in Revelation cannot be very pleasant for those who will witness them.

We may not be able to do much about the tragedies that will come during the last days, but there are some definite steps we can take about our world today. The world's needs are constantly before us—almost nightly on the TV news. Much of the world is in suffering and disaster. We need not sit back and do nothing. There are practical, Christian organizations that are doing something to meet those needs. And we can support those groups and possibly get involved ourselves.

One great world need is to feed the hungry and starving. People who are dying for lack of food care little who feeds them. They will follow any group that has bread and milk. Christians can help fill this gap and prevent many people from dying. We will also help keep them from embracing anti-Christian philosophical and political groups.

Jesus told us, "For I was hungry and you fed me; I was thirsty and you gave me water; I was a stranger and you invited me into your homes" (Matt. 25:35, TLB). He goes on to explain that when we feed and clothe others, we are feeding Him.

A second world need is to educate the illiterate. Those who cannot read must believe those who can. If we reduce illiteracy, we help people to discover the truth.

A third world need is to present Jesus Christ and His grace. Billions are still waiting to hear the Good News. Whole cultures remain untouched by the gospel. Is it any wonder that men whose lives have not been transformed by God's love are still full of hate and anger, greed and vengeance. Feelings of peace for society will not come about when men's lives are full of selfishness and the personal desire to control.

There are answers to the needs of mankind. They are practical and possible. Whether we think of ourselves as hawks or doves, we need not be paralyzed in the fear of the possibility of nuclear war. Helping people seemed like a worthy project to Jesus Christ. He involved himself where the opportunities presented themselves—He transformed people's lives at the most basic levels. So can we. Find out which Christian groups are working in the areas that you see as world needs—support them, pray for them, involve yourself in any opportunity that comes your way.

"Happy are those who strive for peace—they shall be called the sons of God" (Matt. 5:9, TLB).

Love,
Dad

Something to Think About:

1. Do you discuss the possibility of nuclear war at school? If so, what is the opinion of most of the students?
2. What are your thoughts about nuclear weapons build-up?
3. What can you do to feed the poor?

Finding a Church

Dear June,

Do you ever think about what kind of church you would pick out for yourself? Someday that decision will be yours to make. God means for the church to have a dynamic place in your life—the decision needs to be made carefully and enthusiastically.

Let me give a few suggestions to keep in mind. When the time comes, you can weigh them with some of your own and hopefully find just the right congregation for you.

First, find the church where Christ is a member. It is easy for a congregation to get bent out of shape over changing issues like social reform and psychology. Certainly they are important in their place, but beware of churches that have surrendered their first mission: to present and follow Jesus Christ. Christ will lead us to other issues, but beware of any congregation that majors in tangents.

Second, look for a minister who is humble. Some pastors give the appearance that they are the Word of God rather than its messengers. A good minister allows room for disagreement, encourages flexibility in the congregation. Those who take themselves too seriously become rigid, lack compassion and too frequently lose a vital ingredient—a sense of humor. Find a pastor who appreciates the spirit of the law and not just the letter. Seek a minister who can feel and not only teach. Look for love and not judgment. Sit under a pastor who is not afraid to make you think, and does not insist on thinking for you.

Third, join a fellowship where you can lock hands and hearts with others. We need other Christians and all of the strength they can offer. The Bible puts it this way, "Let us not neglect our church meetings, as some people do, but encourage and warn each other" (Heb. 10:25, TLB). A good support group can help you through the rough times and the happy ones, too.

Fourth, don't expect absolute perfection at every level of the church. If people do not measure up to what you expect, if every service doesn't seem to attain to your hopes, remember that church is not a place where we come to be entertained. Church is where we come to share in the life that God has given us. That means we come to give as well as to receive. So, be sure it is a church where you want to jump in and help. You don't need to spend every waking hour there, but you do want to use your talents and gifts to minister to others. Take jobs that are meaningful and serve others. Be creative. Look for places where the congregation hurts and minister in those gaps.

You have a lot to offer. I think you might be amazed how Christ could use you.

Love,
Dad

Something to Think About:

1. What do you like most about your church?
2. How do you wish your church were different?
3. Why do you think your parents chose this church?

Living with a Partner

Dear June,

Despite all the bad publicity marriage gets, most people your age still dream about getting married. It's a good dream because many marriages are successful and millions of couples are getting along great.

You may have reasons to be cautious about marriage, but there are also many reasons to be optimistic. I think if you go the marriage route, you could be happier than a beaver in a lumberyard.

There are no easy steps to a good marriage. If I knew those, we could start a marriage revolution. However, there is one key I believe is especially important. Each marriage partner will have to be ready to change. The inability or unwillingness to change means a couple cannot grow together.

Each of us has habits we have learned to love. But it's impossible to marry and keep all your ways of life exactly the way they are.

That problem has always existed, but I think it used to be easier to deal with. Many people used to assume that it was only the wife's job to change. She was expected to become more like her husband. In recent years women have questioned this. They want to know why they have to do most of the changing.

Why does a woman have to move where the man wants to live? Why does she have to adapt to his timetable and lifestyle? Many women are resisting and saying the changes need to be made by both partners.

The unwillingness for both people to change and adapt may be the number-one problem in young marriages. The change is worth it. Marriage can be a loving, caring partnership, and is for millions.

By remaining flexible with your friends and family,

you could be preparing yourself for a very happy marriage.

"A man must leave his father and mother when he marries, so that he can be perfectly joined to his wife, and the two shall be one" (Eph. 5:31, TLB).

Love,
Dad

Something to Think About:

1. Do you know a couple that has learned flexibility well?
2. What suggestions do you have for a couple about to be married?
3. How can you adapt to your own family better?

When Parents Become Friends

Dear Jim,

Soon we will turn the corner and hopefully enter into a new and even better relationship. It happens to most parents and their teenagers. And I can already see it happening to us. We are reaching the stage where we become friends.

Not that we aren't friendly now, but there is a big difference. Right now I continue to be the authority figure. Sometimes I'm the wall that stands between you and freedom. I won't always be that barrier.

The wall comes down completely when you graduate. Do you want to go on to college? Would you enjoy going into the army? How about being a mountain guide in Nepal? The decision will be up to you. Of course if I can help, I'd like to. However, you can never be a child again. We will be there to listen and suggest and we even may worry and pray, but we are no longer in charge of your life.

We want to be people on whom you can depend. Like good friends we want to share together, do things and go places because we enjoy being with each other. But we don't want to control. If you feel we are trying to control, then let us know; we will back off.

After raising children the purpose is to let them go. Any attempt to keep them as children, manipulate or hold them is counterproductive.

We can still play football on the lawn, have Frisbee wars, even paint doors together. We can still go see Nebraska's Big Red football or watch the Royals in Kansas City. But when we do these things it will be as friends and not just as a parent taking a kid along.

We've certainly had fun. Even when we dumped the canoe in the Illinois River and soaked your watch. Or the time when the crabs got loose in the boat on the Chesapeake Bay. Do you remember sleeping in a damp bunk on a sailboat on the Puget Sound?

Friendship probably sounds far away to you. You would like to fly out of the house and become free. And you will. But don't be surprised if we become friends. Some of the best friendships I see are parents and their children who get together once in a while because they like each other.

You're no longer a kid. Soon you will make the big decisions on your own. When you do, remember that you are guaranteed a friend who cares.

Love,
Dad

Something to Think About:

1. Do you know any father/son friendship or mother/daughter friendships among your adult friends?
2. Do you know any parents who try to control the lives of their grown children? What advice would you give the children?
3. Are you gaining more freedoms as you get older? Enough? Explain.